Classy Knitting

Cartoon by Phil Garland

Dana models her own creation—white sweater

Classy Knitting

A Guide to Creative Sweatering for Beginners

BY FERNE GELLER CONE

Photographs by J. Morton Cone and Ferne Geller Cone

LINE DRAWINGS BY JOANN EVANS

Atheneum   1984   New York

ACKNOWLEDGEMENTS

My sincere thanks to my friends Jane Thompson, Mary Biele and Betty Bell, for lending me their helping hands; to Dana Steele of Campfire Horizon Group, for showing that teens are truly creative and welcome challenges; to Carol Sawyer for a superb typing job; to my special friend, Gladys Nelson, for her journalist's keen eye; to my artist, Joann Evans, for transforming my hen scratchings into drawings; to Gigi Albertson, my young neighbor who modeled so professionally; to Sandra Naon, whose elegance would enhance the simplest design; to my editor, Marcia Marshall, whose enthusiasm and trust I value; and to J. Morton Cone, whose cameras were always ready—any time, any day.

Ferne Geller Cone

Library of Congress Cataloging in Publication Data

Cone, Ferne Geller.   Classy knitting.

SUMMARY: Presents the basic techniques of knitting and guides the beginner in creating an original sweater using simple knits and purls and adding stripes, textures, ribbing, and ruffles.
  1. Knitting—Juvenile literature. 2. Sweaters —Juvenile literature. [1. Knitting. 2. Sweaters. 3. Handicraft] I. Title. TT825.C65 1984   746.9'2   84-2920 ISBN 0-689-31062-5

Published simultaneously in Canada by McClelland & Stewart, Ltd. Composition by Dix Type Inc., Syracuse, New York

Designed by Mary Ahern

For J.M.C.—*who embraces my stitches and strands with complete support, and a marvelous sense of humor.*

F.G.C.

Contents

Classy Knitting

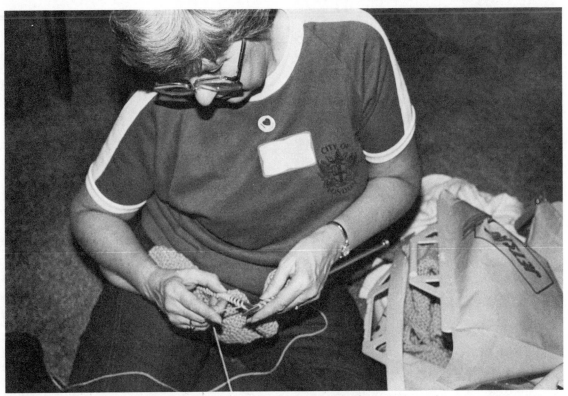

A Campfire "mother" learns to knit along with the girls.

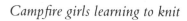
Campfire girls learning to knit

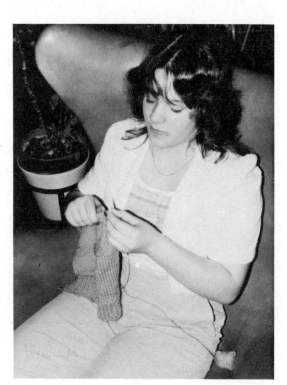

Testing pattern changes

Campfire girl checks her knitting

Introduction

Clothing is a vital part of your daily living experience—no matter what your age. What you wear, and how you wear it, becomes a personal signature. Your appearance, whether or not you will admit it, becomes a transmitter—sending out signals to those around you.

Someone once said". . . a sweater is an extension of the person who made it . . . a pride of individuality." I wholeheartedly agree with that. The big-name fashion designers have finally discovered sweater dressing and have given it their stamp of approval. So now, hand knitting is one of the few fashion alternatives that can be turned into that personal fashion statement. And best of all, it's fun!

Everyone wears sweaters. Remember when you were a little kid and your mother reminded you to put on your sweater? Bet you no longer need reminding. Knits have become status symbols. Everyone wants to get in on the act.

And with the burst of interest in hand knitting, the yarn manufacturers have also finally wised up and are producing gorgeous yarns of unusual textures and color combinations unheard of just a few short years ago. There's something for everyone. If you know how to knit, you'll be way ahead of the game, and save yourself a bundle of money as well.

So, who knits? Rock stars, politicians, ballet dancers, television performers—anyone who really wants to. All over the world people knit. Men and women, teens, little kids. In some countries it's a requirement in elementary school.

For me, it was love at first stitch! Is it easy to learn? Yes, once you learn to handle the needles and yarn. Is it fun? You bet it is, because those interconnected loops on the needles eventually emerge as a real sweater you've created all by yourself. Can you change it? Of course you can. I'll show you how to make it larger or smaller as your measurements change; how to update the design when you tire of the original; and how to apply some decorating tricks that are easy and chic. After you understand how and why things happen, you'll be ready to invent your own designs.

How much will it cost? That will depend on the yarn you choose. Literally, there are hundreds (maybe even thousands) of yarns to choose from, but you'll soon discover that some of the most glamorous yarns can be difficult to work with and the results disappointing. I'll try to help you make wise choices.

There are a million jokes about the little old ladies in tennis shoes, sitting in rocking chairs knitting away. Cartoonists have a field day with knitting. Let them have their fun. Now even teens in tennis shoes know how to knit, and they're turning out gorgeous sweaters, hats, skirts, and many other beautiful knits—to wear and use—and having a great time doing it. You can, too!

To plan this book, I worked with several groups of teens willing to accept my approach. Instead of knitting crazy shapes, or those mundane potholders, they plunged right in and created basic sweaters for themselves. As they began to understand the "why" and "how," everything else fell into place. They realized that they were the boss of the needles and yarn. The fear of making a mistake was immediately forgotten. When they reached that point, there was no stopping their enthusiasm.

The happiest knitters are those who understand how to manipulate shape; then use gorgeous yarns and basic stitches to achieve something out of the ordinary. They have learned how to make the needles behave so they are willing to risk a little.

Therefore, knowing how to put the stitches on and off the needles is only the tip of the iceberg. Keep an open mind, have a little patience and knitting will become a special part of your life, with a lot of pleasure thrown in for good measure.

Later on in the book you'll learn the knitting language, and how to choose an appropriate yarn to work with for your project. We'll also talk about yarn shops and what you may expect from them. (Don't be lured by the trendy yarns—the "jingle and flash.") If you aren't taken seriously, and feel you're being patronized, or not receiving enough information, go somewhere else.

We'll discuss mixing yarns to produce your own color and texture combinations; to use a simple pattern stitch (or combination of stitches), with a basic yarn, and yet make a classy sweater.

Measuring is important. There will be information about taking correct measurements, and how to judge your own figure honestly.

Today, the whole fashion picture emphasizes clothing designs that are soft and fluid—they allow the body to move with ease. We're in a fast-moving culture, and what we put on our bodies has to move fast, too. And that's the beauty and attraction of hand knits—flexibility and style.

Do you already know a little bit about knitting—maybe made a scarf or a hat, but weren't courageous enough to tackle a sweater? I hope this book will provide the incentive to take that extra step. Once you do, you'll become a "yarn junkie" like all of us who have discovered the joy and satisfaction of this special craft.

After you've tackled a sweater or two for yourself, make something for someone in your family, or a sweater for your dog. Use your new skill to make special-occasion gifts for friends. Knitting could also turn into a bonanza for you, if you haven't already thought of it. You could earn extra money by selling what you make. There's a whole treasure trove of ideas for you to explore. Then—teach a friend.

Unraveling the "mystery" of knitting is like unraveling yarn—once it's exposed it's no longer a mystery.

So have a little patience, and spend a little time. Don't say "I can't." Say "I can, I can." You really will.

1

Off and Running

the rules of the road and how to read the traffic signs before you get behind the wheel. Then you practice starting and stopping, going forward and reversing, turning corners, parking. Then you drive around the supermarket parking lot before going out on the streets. Finally, after you've learned to control the car, you're ready for a driver's license. Well, that's how you learn to knit, too. Patience, practice, and a few mistakes. So—first the tools.

To learn the how of knitting, you need only a pair of knitting needles and some yarn. Before that, however, you should know something about the tools and have a nodding acquaintance with the special language. Like driving a car. Before you tear off down the freeway, you learn about the parts and how they function. You learn

The Needles

A few thousand years ago when knitting was invented, people used two little sticks with pointed ends. Since those ancient times, the sticks became needles as we

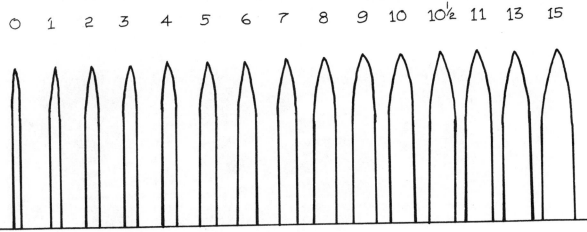

| 0 | 1 | 2 | 3 | 4 | 5 | 6 | 7 | 8 | 9 | 10 | 10½ | 11 | 13 | 15 |

Comparative sizes of knitting needles in U.S.

know them, but now they are made from a variety of materials—aluminum, plastic, nylon and even wood.

There are four types of needles—straight, circular, double-pointed and jumper needles.

STRAIGHT NEEDLES

Straight needles always come in pairs and are the ones you'll use the most. They vary in length from little 7-inch for working with a very small number of stitches, 10-inch for almost all other things, and 14-inch for large numbers of stitches. The 7-inch needles come in sizes "0" to "7," usually made from aluminum. These can be used to knit cuffs, pockets, or anything calling for just a few stitches. The 10-inch needles come in sizes "0" (very skinny) to "15" (fat). They are made from aluminum, nylon-coated metal, and plastic. For beginners I recommend the 10-inch aluminum

needles, in a medium size: 9 or 10. They are easier to work with because they won't bang around and get in your way, and the aluminum is less likely to break. Plastic needles can become brittle in cold climates and snap in two. Plastic and aluminum cost about the same. I personally use 10-inch needles for almost all my knitting projects.

The 14-inch needles range in size from "0" to "50." They are also available in aluminum, nylon-coated metal, plastic, and wood. They're handy when you need to work with lots of stitches. The sizes above "19"—"35" and "50"—look and feel like broomsticks. Unless you plan to make something that calls for combining many strands of yarn at the same time, you probably won't be much interested in these. Take a look at them anyway, just to have an idea of what's available.

Some shops still have wooden needles, usually 14 inches long. These may be used to make garments or other articles requiring open, lacy stitches. They're OK in a pinch, but constant use roughs up the wood—and that's hard on the yarn. I do have a few pairs of wooden needles, which I keep for "emergency rations."

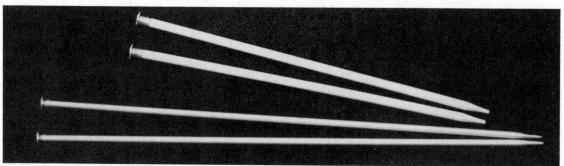

Straight needles

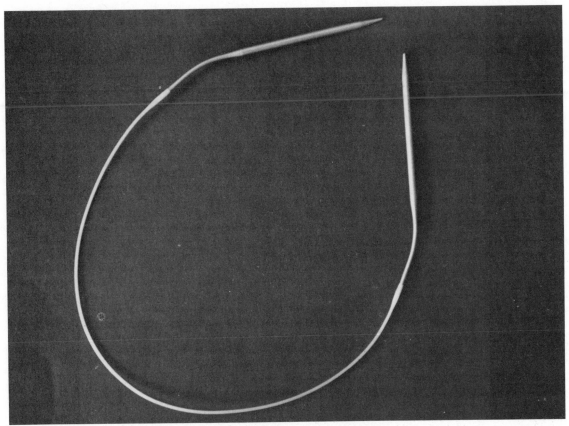

Circular needles

CIRCULAR NEEDLES

The circular needles are designed for working in rounds. They may also be used instead of straight needles for knitting back and forth on a whole bunch of stitches, or for knitting two parts at the same time. Circular needles have two rigid plastic or aluminum pointed ends, connected by a flexible nylon cord. These are available in lengths from 6-inch to 36-inch. The very short ones are used to pick up and work stitches around a neckline, for socks, or for sleeves. The longest circular needles can handle enough stitches for knitting sweaters or skirts without seams. They're much more expensive than straight needles.

DOUBLE-POINTED NEEDLES

Double-pointed needles are also used to work round and round and may be substituted for circular needles. These needles are

Double-pointed needles

pointed at both ends, made from plastic or aluminum. They are packaged in sets of four and are available in sizes up to "11." Somewhat tricky to use, double-pointed needles are necessary should you decide to try socks or gloves where you may need to turn a corner. I hardly ever use them because my fingers always get tangled up in the points. But don't take my word—at least take a look at them. The cost is about the same for either the plastic or aluminum.

JUMPER NEEDLES

Jumper needles are circular needles that look as though they had been cut in half. The points are connected to a flexible nylon cord with a flat disk at the opposite end to prevent the stitches from sliding off. They, too, come in pairs, about 18 inches long, sized from "4" to "15." Jumpers are used just like straight needles and are particularly handy when traveling on planes, trains or buses, where space is tight. They rest easily in your lap so they won't poke your neighbor.

In the United States, knitting needles are sized from "0" the smallest, to "50" the largest. Those made in other English-speaking countries are just reversed—the smaller the number the fatter the needle.

Other Tools

To start knitting you need only a pair of needles and a ball of yarn. However, as you become more experienced, you'll want to add some of the other accessories, too. They're handy to have and quite inexpensive. These include a big-eyed, blunt-point tapestry needle, crochet hook, cloth tape measure, row and stitch counter, point protectors, markers, stitch holders, metal stitch gauge/ruler, embroidery scissors, and T-pins. Some of these accessories you probably already have, but I suggest that before you start your first sweater you should include the scissors, tapestry needle, gauge, tape measure, crochet hook and T-pins. Here are descriptions of these tools to help you identify them when you visit the yarn shop.

NEEDLE AND STITCH GAUGE

This handy tool looks like a 6-inch metal ruler with holes punched in it to measure your needles if you need to. In the middle of the gauge an open 2-inch section is marked off to help you measure the stitch gauge. (More detail about stitch gauge later on.)

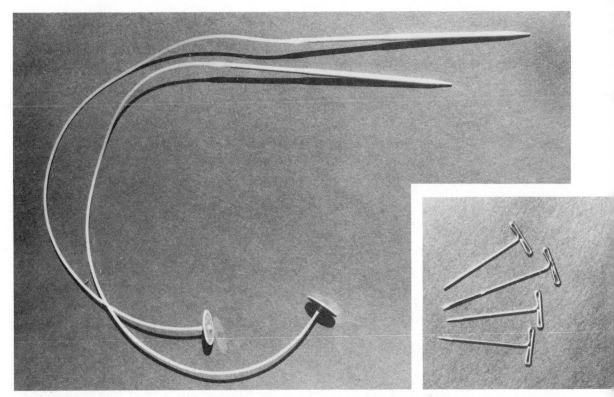

Jumper needles

T-pins

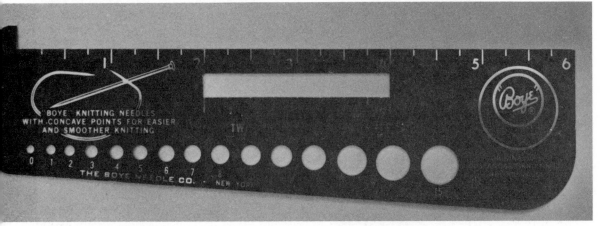

Needle and stitch gauge

In an emergency, substitute a double-pointed needle, a round wooden toothpick, or even a regular safety pin. I've even used a bobby pin when nothing else was handy.

STITCH HOLDER

Many times you'll need to set aside a group of stitches to be worked later. This gadget looks like a safety pin without the coil at the end. You put the stitches on the holder, then work them from the holder directly onto the needle. It's available in several lengths, from mini 2-inch to about 10-inch. You can buy them individually or in sets. It's a good idea to have several sizes.

TAPESTRY NEEDLE

For sewing seams, tacking hems, and connecting other parts, you'll need a blunt-point tapestry needle with an eye big enough so that even a bulky yarn can pass through easily. The blunt point prevents splitting the yarn. No knitter should be without one. They are packaged in sets of two.

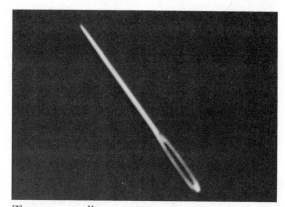

Tapestry needle

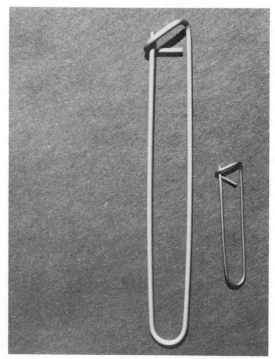

Stitch holders

TAPE MEASURE

A tape measure, preferably a cloth one, should also be a permanent part of your knitting equipment. I advise you to use the same tape measure for all the measurements on your sweaters. This, too, won't make much of a dent in your pocketbook,

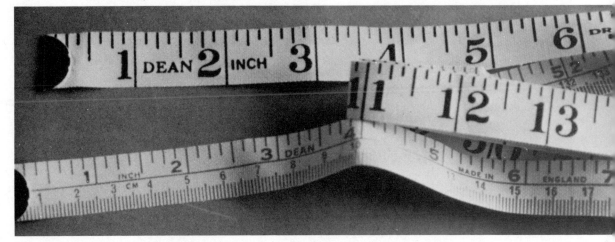

Tape measure

but please, invest in the very best tape measure you can find. Avoid those coiled, spring-type tape measures. They jump around too much to be accurate.

RUBBER POINT PROTECTORS

These little bits of rubber slip over the needle points to prevent the stitches from slid-

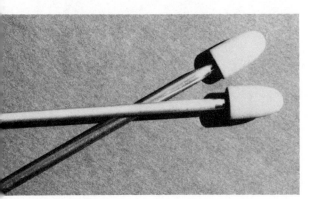

Point protectors

ing off. Not only will they protect the points from nicks and scratches, but will protect you, too, in case you sit on the needles by mistake.

ROW COUNTER

A row counter can be a real help when you need to keep track of the number of rows or have to remember the number of stitches. They're also useful when it's necessary that two parts match exactly, such as sleeves or two sweater fronts. Sometimes it will be necessary to remember the number of stitches and rows at the same time. This little cylinder will help you do that, too.

Row counter

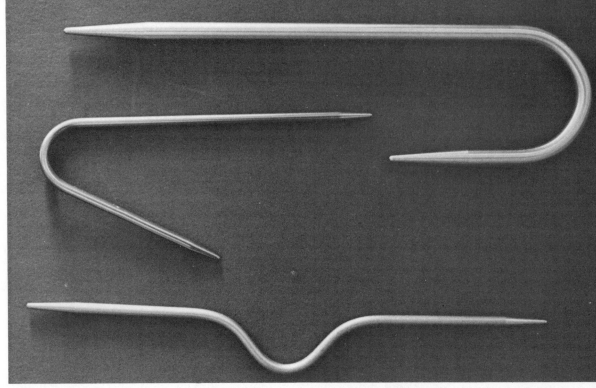

Cable stitch holders

CABLE STITCH HOLDER

As you become more courageous and feel adventurous enough to try some of the cable stitches, you'll want to have a cable holder. There are two types—one that looks like a double-pointed needle bent into a hook at one end, and one that has a bend in the middle. For bulkier yarns, I suggest the hook-type. I use both. The cable holder is designed to keep the stitches out of the way until they're needed to complete the cable. However, here, too, you can substitute a bobby pin.

CROCHET HOOK

A crochet hook is another must. Use it to pick up dropped stitches, for untwisting

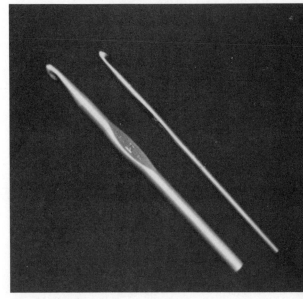

Crochet hooks

stitches, to connect all the parts, or to finish off edges. They're made from plastic, aluminum, and steel. The aluminum and plastic are sized alphabetically from "D" (small) to "K" (large). The steel hooks are sized by number and are usually used for very fine work. I suggest an aluminum hook in a medium size for all-around use. The plastic hooks are easily broken or bent out of shape. Hooks are inexpensive so you may want to have a couple of sizes.

KNITTING CONTAINER

You should keep all your knitting stuff together. Some people use baskets, but unless the basket is lined, you're liable to snag the yarn. A shoebox, or a cloth or plastic bag is better. The plastic bags you get at the supermarket are free—and they are fine.

Small accessories such as markers, T-pins, stitch holders are easily lost or misplaced, so keep them all together in a separate container. Those little ziplock sandwich bags are great for storing these items. Because they're see-through, you'll be able to find what you need without rummaging around.

A few other things to keep handy are an emery board to smooth rough spots on your fingernails so as not to snag the yarn; a notebook and pencil to record special information or to help you keep tabs on what you're doing (or have done); and some short pieces of yarn or string to use as traffic signs in case you need visual reminders. In my workbasket I also keep a small square of toweling for wiping my hands when they become sweaty and sticky.

Knitting Vocabulary

Knitting will be much more enjoyable if you are familiar with the special language and symbols of knitting. Knitting patterns are described by abbreviations. Abbreviations are used mainly to save space because they are often repeated many times within a pattern. Depending upon the book you use, the same technique might be described using different abbreviations. This can really be confusing, especially for a beginner. So in this book everything will be spelled out. Nevertheless, you should become familiar with the most commonly used abbreviations and symbols. Here they are:

K—Knit: putting the needle into the front of the loop on the needle and bringing the yarn around the needle

P—Purl: yarn in front, putting the needle into the loop from back to front and bringing the yarn over and under the needle

St(s)—Stitches: to join the loops by pulling one loop through the other

G st—Garter stitch: knitting every row

St st—Stockinette stitch: knit one row and purl one row

Tog—Together: knitting two stitches together

Co—Cast on: putting the beginning loops on the needle

Bo—Bind off: finishing the knitting by pulling one stitch over another, locking it in place to prevent unraveling

Sl—Slip: to slide a stitch from one needle to the other without working it

Inc—Increase: adding stitches—making two stitches from one

Dec—Decrease: subtracting stitches, working two stitches together—making one stitch from two

Lp—Loop: the folded yarn that forms the basis for all knitting

Beg—Beginning: the start of a row or pattern

K2 tog—Knit 2 together: Knit two stitches together

P2 tog—Purl 2 together: Purl two stitches together

Pat—Pattern: the stitch pattern being used

No—Number: the number of stitches or rows

Psso—To pass a slipped stitch over a worked stitch

Rnd—Round: when working with circular needles equals one row on straight needles

MC—Main color: the prominent color of the garment

CC—Contrasting color: the added color of lesser importance

Kb—Knit back: knit in back of the loop

Pb—Purl back: purl in back of the loop

Rep—Repeat: to repeat the stitch or pattern

Yo—Yarn over: to put the yarn around the needle to make another stitch

Rem—Remaining: the patterns or stitches left to be worked

Symbols:

Asterisk: Asterisks are used to surround a group of stitches or lines in a pattern—★K2tog★

Parentheses: In preplanned knitting patterns additional sizes or stitches are surrounded by parentheses—(12),(14), etc.

Work even: to work without making any changes

If all this seems like a foreign language and you're dying to pick up the needles and yarn, just remember, the more you know in the beginning, the easier the learning.

MORE TIPS

Now that you know a few facts about knitting needles and the other accessories and have a nodding acquaintance with the language of knitting, read this chapter, then do yourself a favor and visit a couple of yarn shops.

Look around at everything. For practice, I suggest you invest in a pair of #10 needles and a ball or skein of *wool* knitting worsted—preferably machine washable. Synthetics are "no-no's" for now. Knitting worsted is about the least expensive and easiest yarn to work with while you learn how to handle the needles. There are at least a hundred colors to choose from, so select one that especially appeals to you. Stay away from very dark colors, such as black or navy. It's too hard to see the stitches, especially at night. I suggest you buy a pair of neutral colored needles for your first pair, so that any color yarn will contrast with the needles.

While browsing around the yarn shop, look at all the other yarns, too. Touch and squeeze them. The many varieties will probably be overwhelming, and certainly beguiling. Just look—don't buy. Not yet. Wait until you have more experience under your belt before trying those gorgeous delicacies, else you'll get in over your head and quickly become discouraged. Soon you'll be skilled enough to indulge yourself. More about yarns later on. For now, all you need to know is that yarns come in prewound balls, ready to use, or hanks or skeins, which you must wind into balls in order to use them.

2

Let's Learn to Knit

You can't wait to get started, so gather up your knitting needles and yarn, find a comfortable chair, be sure the light is good, and let's go!

To knit, you must know only three steps —how to put the beginning loops on the needle; how to use the needle to pull one loop through another to make a stitch; and how to get the stitches off the needle to complete whatever you are making. These three steps are called casting on, knitting, and binding off. *You can learn how in a couple of hours.* After you've learned these three basic steps, we'll talk about increasing or decreasing the number of stitches to make your knitting wider or narrower.

There is no right or wrong way to put the first stitches on the needle. I'll describe two for you. If you already know how to cast on, but your way differs from mine, that's OK. Don't change, unless you want to know some other ways.

Is this the first time you've ever held the needles and yarn? Then you may as well do it my way. The only absolutes in knitting

By the way, I'm teaching you right-handed knitting. You use the muscles in both arms equally, so it doesn't make any difference whether you are right or left-handed. My mother and daughter are very strong lefties, yet they both knit right-handed. I guarantee it won't be a problem for you.

are that you start from a foundation of cast-on stitches, know how to measure the gauge, and how to take the stitches off the needles.

The cast-on loops form the foundation row for the material. There are two basic methods—the one-needle and the two-needle. Both start with a slip knot, which is actually the first stitch.

One Needle Cast-on

For this method measure off a length of yarn about 30 inches long—(you'll use about one inch of yarn for each stitch) and another couple of inches for good measure.

Step 1: Make a slip knot about 4 inches from the cut end (see drawings).
Step 2: Put the loop on one of the needles. This is counted as the first stitch.
Step 3: Hold the needle in your right hand. With the unattached yarn held away from you, put the attached end around your left thumb from back to front.

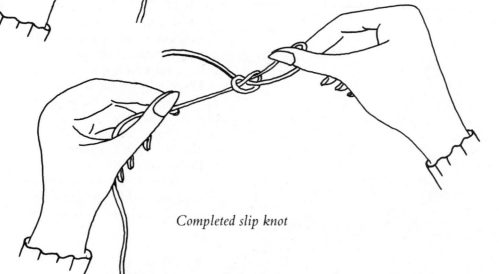

Beginning slip knot

Completed slip knot

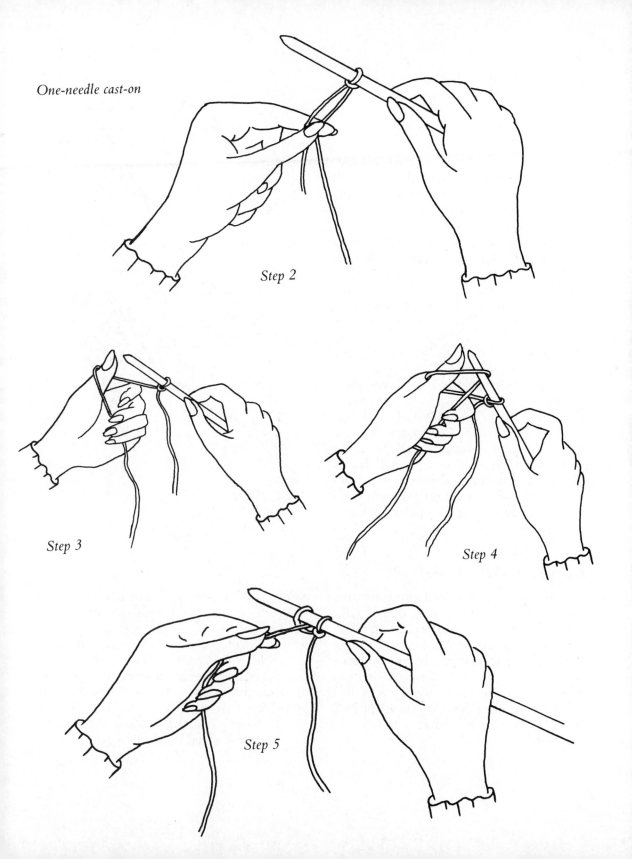

One-needle cast-on

Step 2

Step 3

Step 4

Step 5

Step 4: Place the point of the needle under the yarn in front of your thumb, catch the back strand of yarn with the needle point, pulling it through the loop on your thumb.

Step 5: Carefully slide your thumb out of the loop and tighten the loop on the needle with a little tug on the yarn attached to the ball. There—you've made one loop! Now you have two stitches on the needle.

Repeat steps 2 through 5 until there are 30 loops on the needle.

Some of the stitches will be loose, some tight in the beginning, and you'll probably grip the needles as though you were hanging on for dear life. Not to worry. All new knitters have the same experience. The more you practice the more you'll feel at ease, and casting on will become so automatic you'll soon loosen up. Isn't it always somewhat painful and exasperating learning something new?

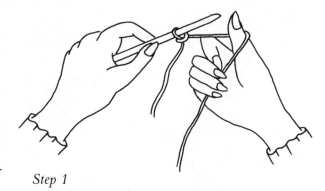

Step 1

Step 2

Two-needle cast-on

Two-Needle Cast-on

This cast-on method actually knits the first row of stitches onto the needle. The edge is looser than the one-needle method. There is a slight advantage—it isn't necessary to anticipate how much yarn to measure off before starting, although it's not quite as fast. Two-needle casting on is used to add stitches for sleeves and to make buttonholes, in addition to the foundation row. Here's how:

Step 1: 4 or 5 inches from the end of the yarn, make a slip knot (see one-needle cast-on).

Step 2: Put the needle in your left hand. Hold the yarn attached to the ball in your right hand and insert the point of the other needle (we'll call this the right needle), from left to right, and through the front of the first loop on the left needle. Notice that the needles are crossed.

Step 3: Pull the yarn under and over the point of the right needle.

Step 4: Draw the loop of yarn toward you through the first loop on the left needle.

Step 5: Put the new loop on the left needle.

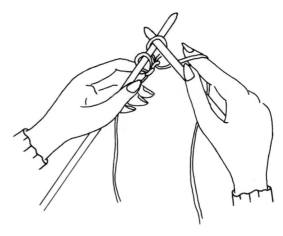

Step 5

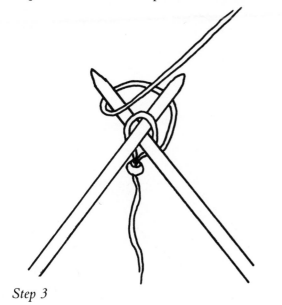

Step 3

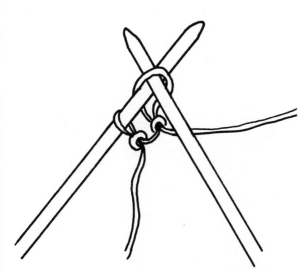

Step 4

You have cast on one stitch and have two loops on the left needle. Repeat steps 2 through 5 until there are 30 stitches on the left needle.

Is it a problem trying to "read" and "do" at the same time? Ask a friend or family member to read each step aloud while you work the needles and yarn. I often do this.

The one-needle cast-on is simpler and faster, so for now concentrate on learning that one. No point in confusing you any more than necessary. Cast on stitches, then pull them off the needle and start over again. Practice until you can do it smoothly.

There are several ways to hold the needles and yarn. I think my way is the most comfortable and least tiring, and you'll have firmer control of the needles. Some other ways may make the knitting go faster. But speed won't make you a better knitter. The important thing is to be comfortable and relaxed.

To Knit

To knit, the loops on the needle are worked back and forth from the left needle to the right needle. Working every row in this manner is called the *garter stitch*. Use the one-needle method to cast on 30 stitches. Leave the needle with the loops in your left hand. This is the left needle.

Step 1: Insert the point of the other needle (right needle) into the front of the first loop of the left needle, from left to right.

Step 2: With your right hand, bring the yarn attached to the ball (working yarn) from back and around the point of the right needle.

Step 3: Holding the yarn and right needle firmly, with the point of the right needle, pull the yarn through the loop.

Step 4: Slip the loop off the left needle.

That wasn't so hard, was it? You've knitted the first stitch! Now the loop is on the right needle. Look carefully at the drawing to see how the working yarn is threaded through the fingers of your right hand. The forefinger is used to pull the yarn over the needles. Keep the yarn moving easily through your fingers to help control tension. Your knitting will be more even. This comes with practice, so don't worry about it now.

Repeat steps 1 through 4 with every loop on the left needle until all the loops have been worked onto the right needle. You've completed one row of knitting. As you work, nudge the loops on the left needle

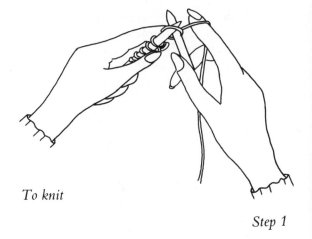

To knit

Step 1

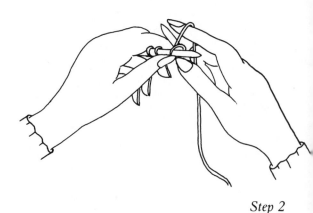

Step 2

toward the point so that the loop you are working is close to the tip of the needle. This will avoid extra strain on the yarn. Careful now—don't push the loop too close to the point or it might slip off.

To knit the next row, put the right needle holding all the worked stitches in your left hand. Again, work each stitch as described above. Each time a row is completed, switch the needle with the worked stitches to your left hand to start the next row.

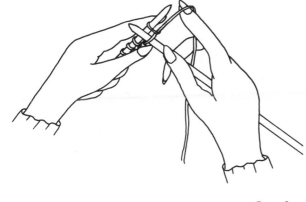

Step 3

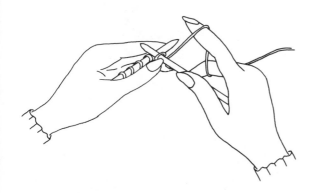

Step 4

and start again. If this seems like drudgery, just visualize all the gorgeous things you can make once you learn to make the needles and yarn do what you want them to do. Each time you start over, those fingers will become more nimble.

Knit back and forth awhile and try not to grip the needles too tightly. Your hands just become sweaty, and it will be a struggle to slide the stitches up and down. Soon the stitches will slide up and down the needles like skaters on ice, and you'll wonder what all the fuss was about.

Before attempting the purl stitch, take a break. Get up and move around—stretch your fingers—have a snack. You'll clear your head and be ready for the next step.

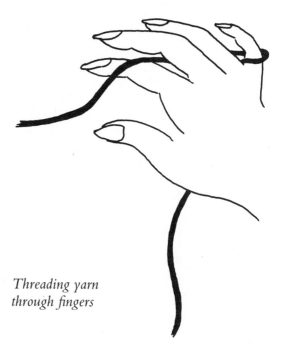

Threading yarn through fingers

To be sure you have the same number of stitches on every row, count the stitches each time you complete a row. Are there more than the original number? You've probably made an extra loop along the way. Examine the stitches. Can you tell where you may have added the extra stitch or stitches? Do you have fewer than the original number? Then you probably dropped a loop along the way, or perhaps you knitted two loops together. This can happen. Grit your teeth, pull the needle out

Garter stitch (detail)

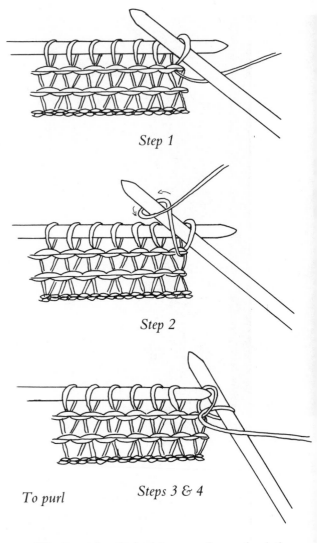

Step 1

Step 2

To purl   *Steps 3 & 4*

To Purl

The purl stitch is the opposite of the knit stitch. The yarn is worked from the front and the needle is put into the stitch from back to front.

Step 1: Put the point of the right needle into the first loop on the left needle from back to front.

Step 2: Pick up the yarn from the front and bring it over and around the point of the right needle.

Step 3: With the tip of the right needle, draw the yarn through the first loop.

Step 4: Slide the first loop off the left needle.

Work each stitch this way from the left needle to the right needle until all the stitches have been worked. To begin the next row, switch the needle holding all the stitches to your left hand, and repeat all the steps.

Purl every row until those movements are familiar. Notice that all the purled rows look like plain knitting on the back side.

Stockinette stitch (detail)

Binding Off

The final step in knitting is called "binding off" . . . sometimes called "casting off." This locks the stitches securely so they won't unravel and is done after all the necessary shaping is finished. There are several other places where you will also bind off stitches—at the armhole, around a neckline, to form a buttonhole, or an insert pocket.

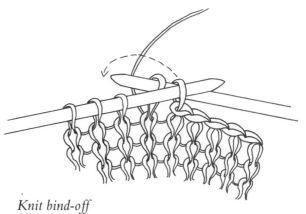

Knit bind-off

You've learned the plain knit and the purl stitch. When the pattern says to work in garter stitch, it means to knit *every* row. A row of *knit* and a row of *purl* is called *stockinette stitch*. The right side of the stockinette stitch is flat and the wrong side is bumpy.

Practice knitting and purling until you are able to recognize one from the other. Work several rows of stockinette stitch, a few rows of garter stitch, a few rows of purl stitch, until you can easily switch from one to the other.

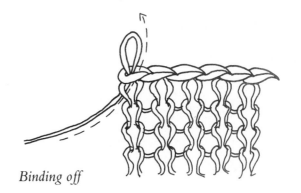

Binding off

KNIT BIND-OFF

On your sample, knit two stitches loosely. With the left needle, pick up the first stitch on the right needle and pull it over the second stitch, and over the point of the right needle. There's one stitch on the right needle. Knit another stitch and repeat the process. Work this way until there is one stitch remaining on the right needle. Leave three or four inches of yarn and cut it. Pull the cut end through the last loop and slip the loop off the needle. All the stitches have been bound off and you've locked in that last stitch.

PURL BIND-OFF

To bind off on the purl side, work the same way except purl each stitch instead of knitting it. Be sure to keep the stitches loose.

Be sure that the bound off stitches are loose enough to move with your material, or else they may pop. After you've done some binding off, you'll be able to have better control.

Should you be working in a **pattern** stitch, bind off in pattern for a neater looking edge. For instance, in working seed stitch—knit 1, purl 1—knit the knit stitch and purl the purl stitch.

Before learning the other stuff about knitting, let's review what you've learned so far.

You know how to cast on and bind off stitches. You've learned how to make a knit stitch and a purl stitch and how to combine them. Are you ready to go on? If you're still a bit shaky and your stitches are uneven, don't worry about it. They'll eventually even up. Let me remind you— the best knitters aren't those whose work looks absolutely perfect, or who are whizzes at knitting pattern stitches, or who knit like machines. The best, and happiest, knitters are those who understand how to manipulate the shape of the material . . . who have control of the needles and yarn, and who are willing to risk and make mistakes in order to accomplish something interesting and individual.

The bottom line is that technical skill, to be sure, is necessary and important. That comes with practice. Common sense and an open mind are equally so.

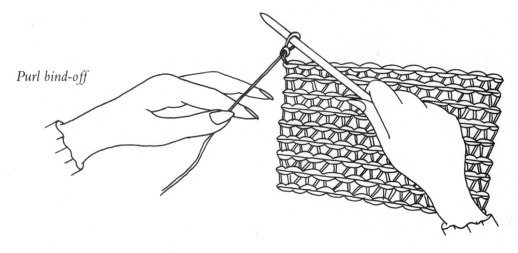

Purl bind-off

3

Increasing and Decreasing

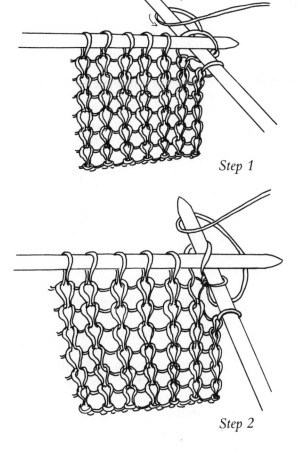

Step 1

Step 2

Hand knitting is shaped by changing the original number of cast-on stitches. To make your work wider, add stitches. To make it narrower, subtract stitches. This is called *increasing* and *decreasing*. Further on in the book we'll discuss when and why you'll need to do this. For now, let's learn *how* the stitches are added or subtracted. We'll start with increasing. Here are four methods:

Simple Increase

This increase is made by knitting first into the front, and then the back of the same stitch. Because it leaves a little bump on the right side of your work, it is usually used at the beginning and end of a row. The bump can be hidden when the parts are connected.

Step 1: At the beginning of the row, knit one stitch. Put the right needle into the

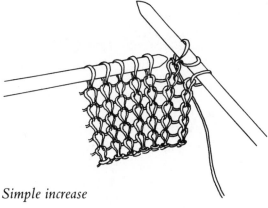

Simple increase

front of the next stitch and knit it the usual way, but leave it on the left needle.

Step 2: Put the point of the right needle into the back of that same stitch and knit it. Slip both stitches from the left needle at the same time.

Knit all the stitches on that row until there is one stitch on the left needle. Repeat steps 1 and 2 in the last stitch.

Preplanned knit patterns will tell you to increase at the beginning and end of a row. What they don't tell you is that if you work the simple increase in the very first stitch, the bump at the beginning will occur at the very edge, but at the end of the row it will occur between the last two stitches. This leaves a lopsided effect. See for yourself what happens. First work the increases as I've described, then work the first increase in the very first stitch of the row. Can you tell the difference?

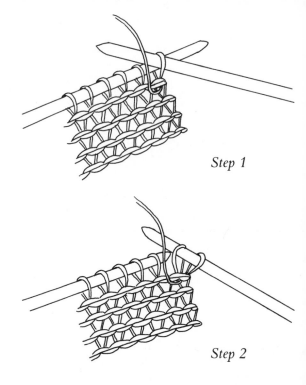

Step 1

Step 2

Purl increase

Purl Increase

Sometimes it will be necessary to increase on the purl side. Here's how:

Step 1: Purl one stitch. With the point of the right needle, pick up the loop below the next stitch on the left needle—from back to front.

Step 2: Draw the working yarn on the right needle to the front and purl the stitch in the usual way.

Step 3: Work a regular purl on the second loop on the left needle.

Back of the Stitch Increase

This is my favorite increase. It's almost invisible and doesn't leave a hole.

Step 1: Knit one stitch. With the point of the right needle, from back to front, pick up the loop on the row below the loop on the left needle and place it on the left needle (notice that the loop is twisted). Knit into the back of the loop.

Step 2: Knit into the back of the original loop on the left needle.

Knit a few stitches and repeat steps 1 and 2. Work this way all across the row. Can you tell the difference between this increase

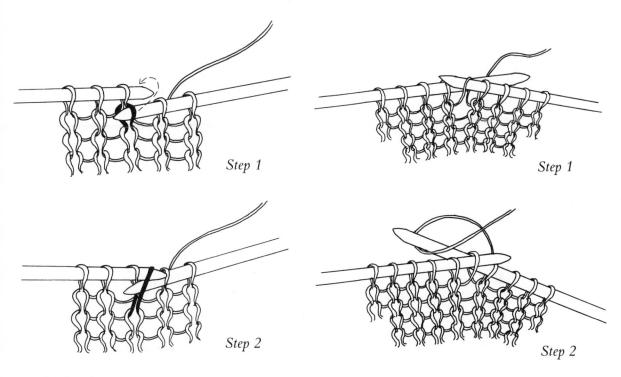

Back of stitch increase

Step 1

Step 2

Row below increase

Step 1

Step 2

and the simple increase? It can be used any-where—at the beginning and end of the row, or right in the middle, and it's hardly noticeable.

Row Below Increase

This increase is made by picking up the horizontal yarn between two stitches. It's easy to do, but watch it to be sure you catch the right strand.

Step 1: Lift the horizontal thread onto the left needle and knit into the back of the lifted loop.
Step 2: Knit the next stitch.

Cast-on Increase

Reread the section (page 18) that describes the 2-needle cast-on for casting on stitches. This increase is mainly used to add several stitches at once, usually at the beginning of a row. It is also used to make buttonholes. Though you've already done this, practice adding stitches this way just to test your memory.

Stitches may be added anywhere—at the beginning or end of a row, at regular inter-vals across a row, or just occasionally somewhere in the middle. As you add more stitches your work becomes wider. Knowing how to use the right increase at the right time will pave the way for a better

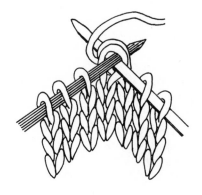

Knit decrease

understanding of the principle of controlling shape. For instance, to make the body of a sweater wider at the bustline than at the waist or hip, you gradually add one stitch at each side instead of all at once. More about control in a later chapter. It's enough for you to know how to make the increases for now.

When you want your work to be narrower in order to shape a particular part of your pattern, it is necessary to *decrease* or subtract from the number of stitches on the needle. In other words, make one stitch from two. You may decrease on either the knit or the purl side.

Sometimes you'll need to decrease at the beginning and end of a row; sometimes all across a row; and sometimes to shape an armhole or a neckline. Here are four ways to decrease:

Simple Knit Decrease

Step 1: Put the point of the right needle into the first two stitches on the left needle, from front to back.
Step 2: Wrap the yarn around as you would to knit, pull it through both stitches at the same time and knit them together. You have made one stitch from two and should have one stitch on the right needle.

Knit a few stitches and repeat steps 1 and 2. Work this way all across the row until two stitches remain on the left needle. Knit the last two stitches together. Knitting the two stitches together in the regular way, from front to back produces a slant to the right. To slant the stitches to the left, knit into the back loops of both stitches at the same time.

Practice these decreases until you can recognize the left and right slant.

Purl Decrease

Step 1: With the yarn in front, insert the point of the right needle from back to front through the first and second loops on the left needle.
Step 2: Wrap the yarn around the needle as you would to purl, pull the yarn through both stitches at the same time, and purl them together.

The idea is exactly the same as decreasing on the knit side except you'll be purling the stitches. Easier than you thought?

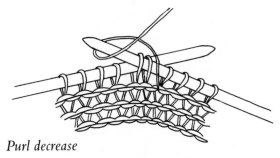

Purl decrease

Slip Stitch Decrease

The slip stitch decrease is referred to as PSSO (pass slipped stitch over) in a commercial knit pattern. Whatever you want to call it, most often it's a decorative decrease, so it's a good one to become familiar with. The PSSO decrease is an obvious decrease not usually made to be hidden, so work it a couple of stitches in from the edge. Done at regular intervals vertically it becomes an attractive border for a raglan sleeve. This decrease slopes to the *left*.

Step 1: Knit two stitches. Slip the next stitch from the left needle to the right needle without working it.

Step 2: Knit the next stitch. With the point of the left needle pull the slipped stitch over the knit stitch, and over the point of the right needle.

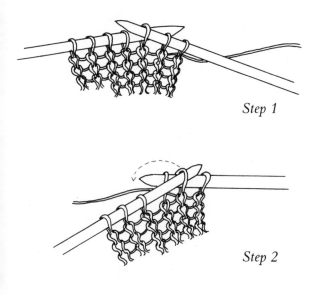

Step 1

Step 2

Slip stitch decrease

The PSSO, or slip stitch decrease is usually worked at the right edge. To balance it, the knit 2 together decrease, which slopes to the right, is worked at the left edge.

It took me a while to discover that knitting 2 together in the back of the stitches, on the right edge, will look the same as PSSO. Do some of these, too, until they become familiar to you.

Using progressively larger or smaller needle sizes is another way to expand or narrow the width of your knitting, *without* adding or subtracting stitches. Try it.

To add width: With #7 needles, cast on 20 stitches. Work 2 inches even. Place a yarn marker or safety pin at one edge. Change to #8 needles and work 2 more inches. Place another marker. Continue knitting and increasing needle size about every 2 inches. Measure the width of each section and record the results in your notebook. As the needle size increases, so does the width of the material.

Reverse the process, and use one size smaller needle every 2 inches, without decreasing the number of stitches. Record the results.

Time to review again, because your head must be whirling about now. Before you tackle more techniques, take another break, then go back and practice everything. Trust me—even if you are still a bit shaky, and the language sounds like a lot of gobbledy-gook, very soon your needles will be flying!

When I first learned to knit, I'm glad I

was curious about all the little twists and turns of the needles and yarn. Why things happened, and what the results might be was never explained. By trial and error I finally realized that my head controlled my hands. I could hide a blooper, or bury it, without endangering the concept. If a shape needed changing, it was OK to change it. Then came the experimenting. Knitting became a challenge and a joy. A whole new world of creativity opened up for me. It will for you, too.

4
The Gauge

One of your best knitting friends is the little 6-inch metal gauge. The other is a good eye. The metal gauge will help you determine the number of stitches to the inch and the number of rows to the inch. This is called "gauge." Your good eye will tell you whether or not your gauge is correct. "Gauge" is the key word. *Engrave it in your memory bank.* Correct gauge can spell the difference between success and disaster—whether or not your garment will fit. There are two types of gauges to be aware of—stitch and row gauge. This is how it works.

Stitch Gauge

Before you start a sweater, you must know how many stitches there are to one inch with the needles and yarn you've selected. The number of stitches per inch can vary by how smoothly and evenly the yarn slides through your fingers. This is called "tension." When you're uptight, you'll grab the needles with a vengeance. Your palms become sweaty, and everything sticks to your fingers. When you are relaxed and comfortable, you won't be inclined to grab those needles as firmly, and the stitches will move smoothly up and down the needles. Make a tension check. The thickness of the yarn and the size of the needles, plus the tension check will help you determine the gauge.

Thumb through some of the pattern books. At the very beginning of the instructions the type of yarn, gauge, and needle size are described. These are determined by the person who knitted that garment. So unless your gauge and needle size are the same, you may need to change the size of your needle to achieve the same gauge. For instance, if the gauge is 4 stitches to the inch on #9 needles, but your gauge is 4½ or 5 stitches to the inch on #9 needles, then you must change to a larger needle. Is your gauge 3 or 3½ stitches to the inch on #9 needles? You should change to a smaller needle. In other words, if you are getting more stitches to the inch, use a larger needle; fewer stitches to the inch, use a smaller needle. Sometimes it's necessary to use a needle two sizes smaller or larger

than the one used in the pattern. What's important is the gauge—not the needle size!

When you design your own sweater and like the appearance of the sample, then all you need do is multiply the number of stitches to the inch by the number of inches for a particular measurement.

I can't stress enough the importance of a correct gauge. Should you get just ½ or 1 stitch more or less per inch, your sweater will be three or four inches wider or narrower.

Let's assume you plan to work with wool knitting worsted and size 9 needles. Cast on 30 stitches and knit about 4 inches. Place the sample on a flat surface (never on your lap). With the metal ruler, measure off two inches horizontally in the *center* of your sample. Place a straight pin at each end of that measurement. The number of

Measuring gauge with stitch gauge

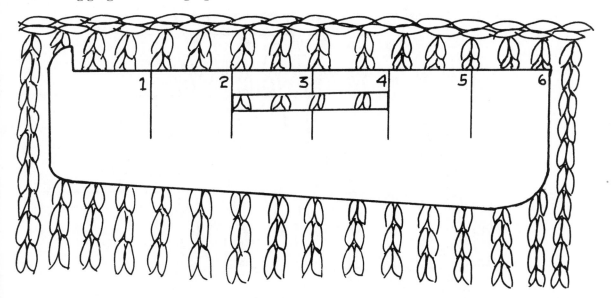

stitches between the pins will be your gauge. Be very careful not to stretch or pull the sample else the gauge will not be a true one and could throw all your calculations off.

For our purposes let's say that the gauge shows 10 stitches equals 2 inches, or 5 stitches to the inch. To determine the number of stitches to begin your sweater, multiply the number of inches of sweater width by the number of stitches in the gauge. If the measurement is 18 inches across, multiply 18 inches by 5, which gives you 90. That's the number of cast-on stitches you'll need. You've determined your own gauge and should maintain that same gauge all the way through. Consistency counts!

As you work, measure the gauge often to be sure the gauge hasn't changed. Does your knitting seem looser than when you started? Better change to smaller needles or try to tighten up. If you have tightened up, change to larger needles and relax. Remember, that extra ½-stitch more or less will completely change the size of your sweater. So be on your guard.

Some people are tight knitters and some are loose knitters. As you gain more experience, your tension will level off and your knitting will be more uniform. Because I'm a tight knitter, I know that when I work from a commercial pattern, I'll automatically use needles at least one size larger than called for in the pattern.

Row Gauge

The "row gauge" is the number of rows to the inch. To find this gauge, lay your metal ruler down the middle of the sample

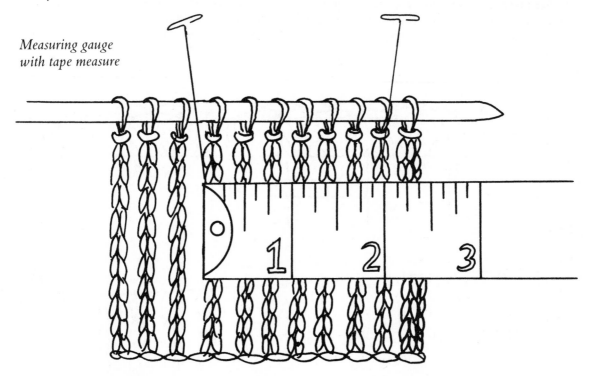

Measuring gauge with tape measure

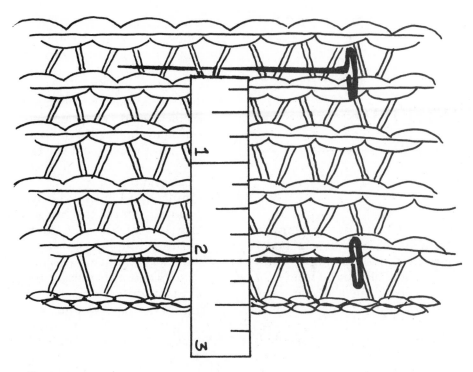

Row gauge

swatch, along the outside edge of a vertical row of stitches. Be sure the ruler is straight along that edge. Place a straight pin horizontally across the top of the ruler, and another pin a couple of inches down. Each stitch equals one row. Do you count 10 stitches between the pins? Then it means there are 10 rows to 2 inches, or 5 rows to the inch.

It isn't necessary to be overly concerned about row gauge, unless a complicated pattern stitch is involved. Vertical measurements are easier to adjust than horizontal measurements. In this book, all the sweater patterns have been designed so that the row gauge is not necessary. But there will be times when you'll need to know the number of rows, so you may as well add this to your learning experience.

Because "gauge" is the key word, perhaps you'd be wise to read this chapter again to be certain it makes sense to you. Are you making notes in your notebook?

When you follow a commercial pattern, be extra careful to be sure your stitch gauge is exactly the same. And for goodness' sake —don't let anyone else work on your knitting! Their intentions may be good, but your knitting will suffer, because rarely do two people ever knit with the same tension and the difference will show in the finished product.

5

Measuring

Before starting that first sweater, draw a little diagram and mark off all your body measurements. Keep this drawing in your knitting bag so it will always be handy. If your measurements change be sure to change the figures in the drawing. Here's how:

There's no need to clutter up your mind with nonessentials now. All the designs in this book are easy-fitting and fluid, so there are just a few necessary measurements to record:

1. Bust: Wrap the tape measure around the fullest part of your bust and all around the back. Put two fingers between the bust and the tape measure for an easy fit. Divide that number in half and record it.
2. Arm length: Underarm (extended arm) to wrist (plus 1 inch for seam).
3. Arm length: Shoulder to wrist (bend arm).
4. Shoulder to hem (from collarbone down and over fullest part of bust).
5. Wrist (at wrist bone).
6. Hip: Wrap tape around widest part of hip with two fingers between hip and tape. Divide that number in half.

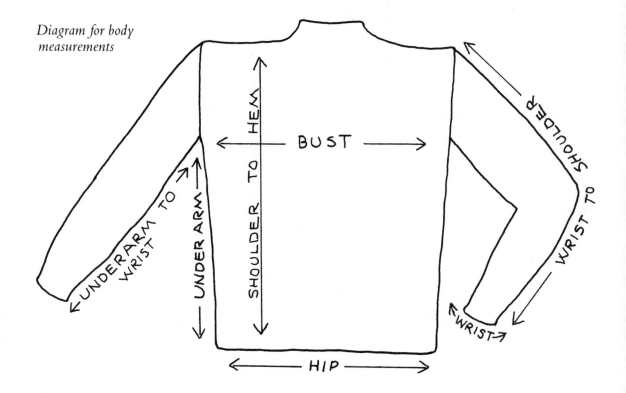

Diagram for body measurements

Have you recorded all these measurements? Now you're ready to start your sweater. We'll use a ball park figure for the hip measurement. Let's say it's 20 inches. You know that your stitch gauge is 5 stitches to the inch, so multiply 20 by 5, 100 stitches. Cast on that number of stitches. If you plan on ribbing at the bottom and at the wrist, use a needle 2 sizes smaller than that for the body of the sweater. Make the ribbing as deep as you like; change to the larger needles and knit until your knitting is the desired length.

Do you have a favorite sweater that fits exactly the way you like it? Use those measurements as a guide.

In the old days, hand-knitted sweaters were designed to fit like a second skin, so the measurements had to be very precise. Even an inch made a big difference. "Comfort" and "movement" describe today's designs, and that extra inch isn't so crucial anymore.

6

Hitches and Glitches

Nobody's perfect. No matter how smart we think we are, mistakes will happen. Despite all the years I've been knitting, I still make some real doozies. Would you believe that I've connected the parts backwards? Once I made two left sides of a sweater because I wasn't thinking. I've even knitted three armholes! More common mistakes are dropped stitches, twisted stitches, working in the wrong direction. I've made all those blunders, too, as have all knitters at one time or another. Don't despair—all these glitches can either be corrected or disguised, without anyone except you being the wiser. As a matter of fact, miscalculations can often turn a mistake into an even more interesting detail. A famous person once said . . . "mistakes are to learn from, not to cry over." Think about it.

Most mistakes happen when you're not paying attention, or are in a rush. To be on the safe side, learn how to recognize and correct these hitches and glitches.

Dropped Stitch

You've dropped a stitch—it slipped off the needle before you could catch it and it crawled down a couple of rows. Quick! Grab your crochet hook and put the hooked end through the loop. Now it's safe and won't unravel any further. For stockinette stitch, with the right side of the work facing you, carefully remove the hook and slide it into the front of the dropped loop. Catch the first horizontal thread just above that maverick loop and pull it through the loop. Work this way back up to the needle. Put the loop back on the needle. Be sure the stitch is facing in the same direction as all the other stitches on the needle. Pick up a dropped purl stitch from the other side.

Dropped pattern stitches are difficult to pick up. Better to unravel back to the dropped stitch.

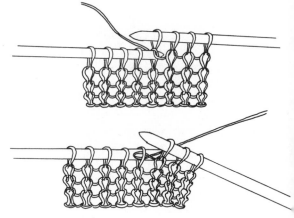

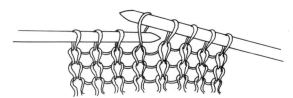

Undoing stiches

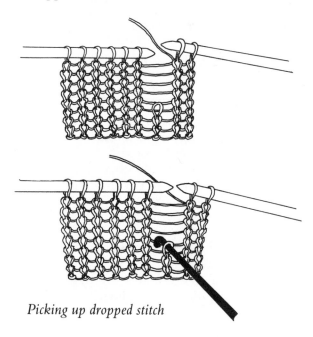

Untwisting a stitch

Picking up dropped stitch

Twisted Stitches

You weren't paying attention, and somewhere along the row you knitted into the back of the stitch instead of the front. It's twisted, and it shows. Don't cry. It isn't necessary to pull the needles out. You can undo stitch by stitch until you work back to the twisted stitch. Here's how: put the point of the left needle into the loop *below* the first stitch on the right needle, from front to back. Slip that loop onto the left needle. At the same time, the loop from the right needle will automatically slide off. Make sure the loop on the left needle is not twisted. Work back this way to the twisted stitch. Untwist it, then continue working. You're wiser to undo stitches one by one rather than pulling the work off the needles, if you discover the mistake before you start the next row. You're too apt to unravel the stitches by pulling them off the needle.

As you undo the stitches, be sure all the loops face in the same direction. The knitted stitches will slope from left to right, and the twisted stitches will slope from right to left.

Knitting in the Wrong Direction

You're happily knitting away, but before the row is completed, the telephone rings, or a friend stops by. You put your knitting aside. When you pick it up again, in the haste to get going, you've started in the wrong direction, and there's a big hole. Use the same method to correct this mistake as described in the section on twisted stitches.

To avoid this in the future, remember that the working yarn is always on the right needle. If that isn't enough of a reminder, place a safety pin just below the first stitch on the right needle. When you pick up your knitting again, the pin will tell you which way to start knitting.

Lost Stitch

Another common mistake knitters make at one time or another is to drop a stitch without even being aware of it until several inches have been knitted. What to do?

Well, brace yourself and be prepared now to pull the needles out and unravel the knitting back down to the row just *above* that runaway stitch. Then rip back stitch by stitch, as I've already described, to the mistake. Pick up the dropped stitch and put it back on the left needle, and continue knitting.

It would have been so helpful if someone had shown me how to recognize and correct errors when I learned to knit. Not knowing what you're doing, or why you're doing it can be frustrating enough to turn you off knitting, and that would be a shame! So much of what I've uncovered about knitting was discovered by trial and error. That's not altogether a bad way to learn, but it can waste a lot of time fiddling around.

The Great Cover-up

Here are a few suggestions that might come in handy for hiding mistakes that eluded you before you put all the pieces together. I've seen some beautiful hand knits made from expensive yarns, with big, glaring mistakes right smack in the middle! I always wondered why the knitter hadn't at least made an effort to correct that clinker before finishing the sweater, or at least to find a way to disguise it.

I promised to give you some cover-up tips, so here they are. For instance, let's assume that a mistake occurred in the body of the sweater where it's sure to show . . .

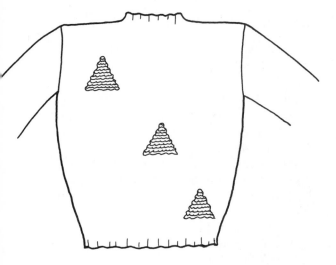

Knitted cover-up—triangles

perhaps you knitted but should have purled. But you didn't notice the mistake until the sweater was all finished. Knit a triangle or square from the same or contrasting color, and sew it right on top of the mistake. Does this look too obvious? Make several triangles and/or squares and sew them at random all over the sweater. That's one idea. If you don't have enough yarn to do that, buy a package of ready-made appliques and sew them on the same way. They cost about $1.00

Here are some other possibilities. When you tire of the knitted patches, they may be easily removed and replaced with knitted stripes. Make the stripes in different lengths and/or widths, and sew them on with matching yarn.

Lightning strips made with bias knitting (see page 89) can be fun, too. Appliqued horizontally, vertically or diagonally, they will cover up the error and add a touch of "flash" to your sweater.

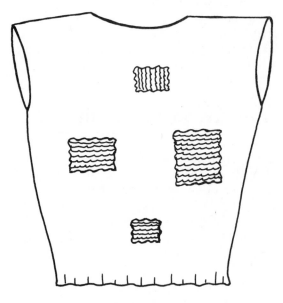

Knitted cover-up—squares

Knitted cover-up—stripes

I suggest you use a garter stitch for all these tricks because the edges remain nice and flat and easy to sew.

Now that I've given you a few of my cover-up tricks, think of other ways to mask that mistake—put your imagination to work!

Before starting your first sweater—I know you're anxious to get going—deliberately make and correct these mistakes. Test yourself. When any of these glitches and hitches happen in the middle of your project, you'll know what to do. As a reminder, make some notes in your notebook, and refer to them when necessary.

7

Picking Up Stitches

There will be many times when it is more effective to pick up stitches—around the neckline on a sweater, along an edge, or to add some surface interest (see directions for Big Shirt). Try this on your sample first. We'll start with edge stitches. Put the point of the right needle into the first stitch of the right edge. Leaving a short end of the new yarn (working yarn), catch the new yarn with the needle point and pull it through that first edge stitch. This automatically forms a loop on the needle. It is

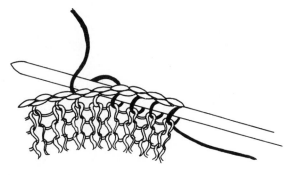

Picking up stitches at edge

not knitted on. That's the first picked-up stitch. Repeat this through each stitch along the edge. After the required number of new loops are on the needle, knit or purl as you normally would.

To pick up stitches on the surface of your knitting, fold the knitting along one row of stitches to be sure all the picked-up stitches form a straight line. Put the point of the right needle into the horizontal thread behind the stitch, catch the yarn and pull it through. Work this way until the required number of stitches have been picked up. Continue knitting.

In side-to-side knitting (page 98) ribbing is formed by picking up stitches along the bottom edge and working vertically.

To add width to a sweater, undo the side and underarm seams, and pick up stitches along the seam edge.

8

Starting New Yarn

Inevitably you reach the end of the yarn and have to start a new ball. How? There are many schools of thought about how to do it. Most insist that the new yarn only be connected at the beginning or end of a row. If you have plenty of yarn and aren't worried about using up a bit more, then that's the way to go.

As you come near the end of the ball, measure the remainder of the yarn. You should have about 3½ times the length of

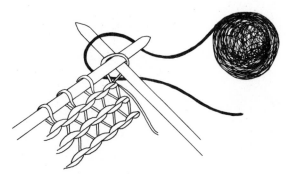

Starting new yarn at beginning of row

the row to finish it. If not, rip back to the beginning of the row and start the new ball. You'll probably have many inches of extra yarn dangling along the side. However, since I hate waste, I will start the new yarn wherever the old one ends, except when changing color, or if I'm working an open stitch. So, if you're nervous about the small amount of yarn and don't want to waste even an inch, it's all right to start a new yarn anywhere along the row.

To start the new yarn at the edge of your work, drop the old yarn, leave about 4 inches of the new yarn, and continue knitting with the new yarn. Knit a couple of rows, then go back and tighten up the loose ends. To keep them from getting tangled up in your knitting, tie those ends in a single knot. This is temporary. When you sew the two edges together, the ends will automatically be secured. Then you can untie the temporary knot and the bump won't show on the right side of your work. (See Loose Ends)

To connect the new yarn in the middle of a row, work to within three or four inches of the old yarn. Lay the new yarn across the back of your needle, with the end of the new yarn facing the opposite direction. With the double strand, knit 2 or 3 stitches, drop the old yarn and continue working. The few stitches knitted with 2 strands of yarn will never show on the right side, and the new yarn is securely locked into your fabric. I call this "splicing."

Knots are "no-no's." You can't hide them. Eventually they'll pop through or work loose as you wear the sweater, so avoid them, except as a temporary measure at the side of your work.

There are two exceptions to splicing: one, when joining a new color (the two different colors will look like tweed and certainly be noticeable); two, when working an open pattern stitch. If either of these situations occur, join the new ball at a side edge.

You should be familiar with both types of joinings, so don't forget to practice.

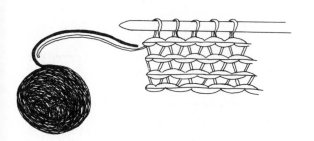
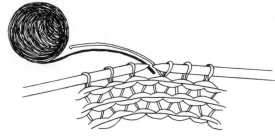

Splicing yarn

9

Stitches and Strands

All pattern stitches are combinations of the basic knit and purl. The way the yarn is manipulated around the needles provides all the pattern stitch variations. I have strong opinions about using pattern stitches. To me, there's a tendency to "overkill" with pattern. I'm inclined to use them sparingly—when a touch of pattern will add zest to the shape of the garment, or when an overall simple pattern stitch will enhance the design.

Commercial patterns tend to rely on a bunch of pattern stitches to carry the weight of the design. This overdosing can date the garment very quickly. Having to remember all those twists and turns bores me silly; besides, I have a rotten memory. Yarns are pricey, and time is precious. Few of us can afford to indulge in whimsy.

Yet it is fun to try pattern stitches, just to see if you can follow the directions, or if you enjoy the process. Should you choose a complicated stitch, think long-term, and ask yourself these questions: "Is it fun to do?" "Is it hard to follow?" "Will it en-

hance the design?" "Can I live with it for a long time?" "Do I have the patience to keep track of the different rows?"

Because my attention span is limited, I'm not enamored of any pattern stitch that includes more than a few lines to complete the pattern. It's not my style. But it may be yours. It's been recommended that transferring the directions to a series of file cards makes it easier to follow the directions. I've done that, too. But the constant flip-flop from card to needles gives me a headache. In a true fashion sense, the shape of the garment and color and texture of the yarn is much more vital for a truly smashing result.

Don't let me turn you off pattern stitches. This is something you should decide for yourself. Follow the directions for the stitches I've included in this chapter. They were especially selected for their adaptability and ease. Then you can pick and choose those you most enjoy. Many books that contain more complicated stitches are available, so when you are in the mood to experiment further, look them over and give them a whirl.

Ribbing

Ribbing is elastic, so it's used most often for cuffs and hems and around necklines. Frequently it is effective as an all-over pattern for a more form-fitting sweater. Add a strip or two of ribbing down the center of your sweater to break up the monotony of stockinette stitch. Repeat it down the center of the sleeve. Alternate 2-inch horizontal stripes of ribbing with garter or stockinette stitch. Other ways to use this very simple stitch will occur to you as you become more experienced.

Four ribbing pattern stitches are described for you to try: Knit 1, purl 1; knit 2, purl 2; knit 1 in back, purl 1; knit 2 in back, purl 2.

All of these variations are worked with an even number of stitches. They all start with a knit stitch and end with a purl stitch. Each time you change from the knit stitch to the purl stitch, the yarn is brought forward. Bring the yarn back to change to the knit stitch. When ending the row with a purl stitch always start the next row with a knit stitch. Notice that the purl stitch on one side is the knit stitch on the other side.

Ribbing looks the same on both sides . . . like railroad tracks with indentations in between. Used with the same number of stitches as in the body of your sweater, they will automatically pull the fabric closer to your body. For a more distinct division, try a smaller size needle for the ribbing, then change to the larger needles.

Ribbing has plenty of depth, so I recommend using a flat rather than a textured yarn.

Lacy, open-pattern stitches are fun to play with. They require concentration, so try these when there are no distractions around. Open stitches are usually made with "yarn overs." If you lose the yarn over, or put it in the wrong place, it's better to unravel that row than try to fix it. I've spent too much time trying to correct an open stitch when it would have been simpler to unravel.

The yarn over (sometimes called a "make" stitch) will add a loop on one row, increasing the number of stitches on that row. On the next row of the pattern it will tell you to "knit 2 together." This cancels out the added loop. You'll end with the original number of stitches.

These lacy stitches are especially interesting when used as an all-over pattern made from cotton or linen yarn. They also are adaptable as pattern blocks.

Included in this chapter are a couple of fabric stitches that I like to use for outerwear such as jackets or coats. They produce a solid, textured fabric, so keep this in mind when choosing the yarn and sweater design.

Pattern stitches generally use up more yarn than garter or stockinette stitch. The stitch gauge may change (unless you insert such a small section that the difference won't affect the fit). For instance, ribbing uses up about 1½ times as much yarn as garter or stockinette stitch.

An open stitch won't necessarily require more yarn—sometimes less. But it could expand the material. Be extra careful when measuring gauge.

Experiment before making a final decision. Work each of the pattern stitches in this chapter on one size needles. Can you follow the directions? Work them on different sizes of needles. Notice that each time you change needle size the pattern changes slightly. Record your reactions in your notebook. This testing time is valuable because it may bring forth some little detail you had not anticipated.

Single rib

SINGLE RIB

The single rib is the most commonly used ribbing for edges on sweaters, jackets, necklines and sleeves. It is effective, also, as an allover pattern stitch.

Cast on an even number of stitches.

Row 1 (and all other rows): ★Knit 1, purl 1.★ Repeat these two stitches between the ★★ to the end of the row. End with purl 1. Work to desired length.

DOUBLE RIB

This is the double version of the single rib. It is also worked on an even number of stitches that can be divided by 4.

Row 1 (and all other rows): ★Knit 2, purl 2.★ Repeat these 4 stitches between the ★★ to the end of the row. End with purl 2. Work to desired length.

Double rib

SINGLE TWISTED RIB

The single twisted rib is exactly the same as the single rib, except you will knit into the *back* of the knit stitch. This twisted rib is firmer than the conventional rib, but can be used the same way. The texture is more prominent.

Cast on an even number of stitches.
Row 1: ★Knit 1 in back, purl 1★. End with purl 1.

Single twisted rib

Stamen stitch

Double twisted rib

DOUBLE TWISTED RIB

Cast on even number of stitches that can be divided by 4.

Row 1: ★Knit 2 in back, purl 2★. Repeat these four stitches between the ★★ to the end of the row. End with purl 2.

Stamen Stitch

This stitch is best worked with flat knitting worsted or lighter weight yarn so the true effect of the pattern will show. It also makes an attractive border around a neckline, inserted along the side of a sweater, or

anywhere else you please. Be alert when working this stitch because the slipped stitches might fool you.
Cast on an even number of stitches.

Row 1: Knit all across the row.
Row 2: ★Knit 1, slip 1 stitch as if to purl★. End row with knit 2 stitches.
Row 3: Knit across the row.
Row 4: Knit 2, ★slip 1 stitch as if to purl, knit 1★.

The photo (on page 45) shows this stitch knitted on # 9 and #11 needles. Can you tell how the texture changes with the different needles? The weave is quite dense, so it would be especially practical for a jacket or coat sweater. Combine it with a single ribbed hem and cuffs, and you'll have a very handsome, warm, pullover.

Sand Stitch

The sand stitch is a combination of plain knitting and knit 1, purl 1 ribbing, which makes a nubby texture. Both sides of the pattern are equally interesting, so you have a choice. There are just two rows to this pattern, and it is easy to remember; but be sure not to mix them up. Practice this one for a couple of inches until you are able to recognize the two rows.
Cast on an even number of stitches.

Row 1: Knit every stitch.
Row 2: ★Knit 1 stitch, purl 1 stitch★. Re-

Sand stitch—right side

Back side

peat the stitches between the ★★ all across the row. End with purl 1 stitch.

The photos above show both sides of the fabric.

Turkish Stitch

Here's your introduction to a simple lacy stitch. It has just one row to the pattern worked on an even number of stitches, re-

Turkish stitch

peated every row. It's especially attractive worked on larger needles with a medium-weight yarn. But equally so worked on medium size needles with bulkier yarn. The yarn over makes a new stitch; the knit 2 together eliminates a stitch. One balances the other, so you always end with the same number of stitches on every row. As you work this stitch, pay particular attention to the slant of the yarn-over stitch. It slants to the left.

After you practice this version, instead of working every row in the pattern, work one row in pattern and one row of plain knit. Then try it with one row of pattern and one row of purl stitch. It's really fun to do, but watch it to be sure those yarn overs don't get lost.

Cast on an even number of stitches.

Row 1: Knit 1, *yarnover, knit 2 together: repeat from *. End with a knit 1. Repeat row 1 on every row.

Seed Stitch (sometimes called Rice Stitch)

This stitch produces a little bit of texture and looks the same on both sides. It's often used for borders because the fabric is rather firm and stays nice and flat. Actually the seed stitch is the same as the single rib stitch, except that on the second row, the knit stitch occurs just above the purl stitch on the preceding row, and the purl stitch is above the knit stitch.

Cast on an even number of stitches.

Row 1: *Knit 1, purl 1*. Repeat stitches between ** across the row. End with purl 1.

Row 2: *Purl 1, knit 1*. Repeat stitches between ** across the row. End with knit 1.

Seed stitch

Stockinette and reverse stockinette stitch combined two ways

There are literally thousands of knit pattern stitches. I've chosen these few because they will provide experience in following a pattern. They will also help you to understand how to manipulate needles in order to change the texture of your knitting. When you look through other books that concentrate on pattern stitches, you may discover different names for some of the pattern stitches, which could be confusing. Eventually, as you build up your knitting skills, you'll be able to recognize the stitches themselves.

Don't try to be an expert right away. But I urge you not to be timid about trying something different. If you goof, what's the very worst that could happen? Well, you may have to unravel. It's not the end of the world. Don't be discouraged. Cast on a new bunch of stitches and try again.

Try each of these pattern stitches with various sizes of needles and watch how they change and grow. Then combine some of them, just to play around. Some you may enjoy, but others will turn you off. Give them a spin and see how creative you can be. Remember, all the pattern stitches in all those knitting books were originally invented by someone playing with the stitches. Who knows, you may invent a new stitch of your very own!

10

The Right Choice

Now comes the really exciting part of knitting—choosing the yarn. Naturally, the stitches are important, but I want to stress again that you work with the very best quality of yarn you can afford. Why toss out time and effort on inferior material? Today, there are so many choices, color- and texture-wise, that it's almost an embarrassment of riches . . . and confusing as well. There are pure wools, linens, cottons, synthetics, silk and rayon—and combinations of all of these.

Knitters used to have few choices—yarns were dull, color choices limited, and styles uninviting. Some creative knitters made up their own combinations. Then the yarn manufacturers finally saw the handwriting on the wall. They began to produce exciting textures, with almost unlimited color choices. Fashion designers are using yarns in a whole new way. You can, too. Hand knitting has achieved important status in the fashion world and the possibilities are incredible!

Don't even think about starting your

first sweater until you shop around. Touch and feel everything, and be sure to read the labels. Most yarn shops will have samples on display so you can see how each yarn will look when knitted. This is very helpful, especially for beginners, because it's difficult to tell what a yarn will look like *until* it's knitted. Yarns can be deceiving, so ask lots of questions.

Knitting yarns are available in hanks or skeins (which you have to wind into balls yourself), or in prewound balls. All are labeled, and these labels contain *very important* information. The label will tell you what the yarn is made of (wool, cotton, linen, synthetic, or the percentage of combinations). Each label indicates a color and dye lot number. Pay special attention to this information. The color number might read "Col. 8" (this could be a yellow), the dye lot number 1542. Therefore, it means that Color 8 has been reproduced 1542 times. If you start your sweater with Color 8, dye lot 1542, buy *enough* of that dye lot to finish your sweater, plus an extra ball or two in case you decide to change some detail, or lengthen it. You may not be able to match the dye lot next time. Check the label on each ball or skein to be sure they're the same. Whites and blacks are especially tricky—so watch out.

Other important information is usually included, too, such as laundering or dry cleaning instructions, the number of ounces or grams, the recommended needle size and stitches to the inch, and whether the yarn has been preshrunk or moth-proofed. Some labels also include the approximate number of yards.

I wish there were some consistency to the information that appears on yarn labels. Life would certainly be easier for all knitters. Because so many of the new yarns are manufactured in other countries and only distributed in the United States, this is hard to control. Anyway, we're happy to have the information that is available, so please do take it seriously. Many hours will be saved by reading and digesting those details *before* you make a selection.

What's "in" today may be "out" tomorrow. No matter how tantalizing some of those gorgeous, glitzy yarns may be, go easy the first time out. Don't get carried away by the flashy fibers. Have some fun with color, but stay away from the bumpy, or fuzzy yarns—at first—until you have knitted a couple of sweaters.

Some knitters can be too chintzy about yarn. They hate to buy even one extra ball

An embarrassment of riches

or skein. That's poor thinking. When they run out of yarn, or a hole needs repairing, or they decide to change the design, they could be up a creek. It's happened to me. After a couple of these traumatic experiences, I always have that extra yarn, for just in case.

On the bright side, if you do run out of yarn before the sweater is finished, and no more is available, tap your creative juices. You may have to add a stripe, even though you hadn't planned one. Perhaps you've decided midstream to make the sweater longer than the original design. Here's where your originality will blossom forth.

Occasionally a knot or two will occur in commercial yarns where it was necessary to connect a new strand. When this happens, break the yarn at the knot. Then connect the two ends as described on page 41.

One, maybe two, knots are acceptable. Any more and I consider the yarn defective and unacceptable. Return it to the yarn shop for a replacement.

Are you concerned about having a whole bunch of leftover yarns? Don't be. Some of the patterns in this book show how to use them in interesting ways—for other wearables or for hand knits to decorate your room.

Most yarn shops will have a lay-away policy—you can buy half the amount, and the shop will keep the rest for you—usually 60 days. But you say you can't possibly finish in 60 days? Here's a formula that I find pretty reliable. Buy one ball or skein and ask to have the rest saved. Knit a sample swatch for gauge and needle size in the pattern stitch you intend using. Start with the sweater back. For example, if you have a hip measurement from side to side of 20 inches, and a gauge of 5 stitches to the

inch, then you already know to cast on 100 stitches. Knit up that one whole ball of yarn.

For our purposes, let's say one ball works up 6 inches of fabric. Therefore, if one ball or skein of yarn produces a piece 20 inches wide and 6 inches deep, and the measurement is 18 inches from shoulder to hem, you would need 3 balls of yarn for that section. Assuming that the front is about the same as the back, 3 more balls are needed for the front. For 2 long sleeves, 1½ balls each should be ample. Altogether, 9 balls of yarn should do it. To plan a cardigan, another half ball will be necessary to take care of the button overlap. Then add one more ball as a security blanket. Depending on how you like your sweaters to fit, this is a rather generous calculation, but at least you won't run out of yarn right in the middle. Perhaps you may even have enough left over to knit a matching hat and/or matching head band. Surely enough to patch up holes or make alterations at some future time.

Today's relaxed, unstructured, straight-line sweaters use more yarn, but they're smashing as well as comfortable, so why quibble about one ball of yarn. Consider it a wise investment.

In earlier days, a rough rule of thumb for calculating the correct amount of yarn for a basic sweater was about four times as much yarn as necessary for the back. This is based on those close-fitting designs. If you used two 4-ounce balls of knitting worsted for the back, then probably 8 balls would be about right to complete the sweater.

Whether you plan to create your own design, or follow a printed pattern, keep the leftovers with one of the labels, and put them in a safe place. Check the label again before washing or dry cleaning your sweater.

There are too many yarns available today to describe each one. However, they include yarns of wool, cotton, linen, rayon, nylon, countless other synthetics, and combinations of some or all of these.

Pure wool yarn is a natural fiber. It has always been, and still is, my favorite. I hope it will be for you, too. You will appreciate its elasticity, the wide range and purity of colors and textures, the wearability, and, of course, the warmth. Some wools are smooth, some crinkly, some are fat, some thin, some both thick and thin. Even if it sounds like a broken record, I'll repeat it again—knit your first couple of sweaters from a basic flat wool, such as knitting worsted. You'll easily be able to see the stitches. It goes a long way and is about the least expensive. Wool is easy to combine with other yarns, and it always springs back into shape.

Other natural fibers include linen and cotton. They are very strong and will last a long time. These must be knitted to fit because they have no elasticity, but they are easy to care for and launder beautifully. Linen and cotton yarns are now being manufactured in marvelous colors in a variety of textures. They're great for summer sweaters. Knit a few sweaters before you try these.

And then there are the synthetic or man-made yarns. Some of the new synthetics are most intriguing. In some cases it's almost impossible to tell the difference between the synthetic and the real thing. There are as many variations of these yarns as there are the naturals. However, there are some drawbacks about using synthetics that you should be aware of.

Although advertised as easy-care (they may be tossed in the washing machine and dryer), sometimes they may be more trouble than they're worth. After a few wearings they begin to pill, and stains may be more difficult to remove. They do not hold shape, either.

There's no fooling around with synthetic yarns—they must be knitted to fit. Should you need to unravel, the kinks are permanently set so they're always obvious. Heat and synthetics don't get along, either. Intense heat will literally melt the yarn— even body heat can cause the fibers to relax and stretch out of shape, as will water.

My prejudice against synthetic yarns is showing. Sorry. Just because they're not my cup of tea doesn't mean you should ignore man-made fibers. Try a skein or two to see how (or if) you like them. But keep in mind potential problems.

Commercial patterns usually recommend a specific yarn. The stitch gauge and needle size have been developed to suit that yarn. However, you can substitute one yarn for another, providing the fiber content and stitch gauge are the same. Ask for guidance in making substitutions. *McCall's Needlework* publishes an "Interchangeable Yarn Chart" listing the majority of yarns manufactured and their interchangeable features. You can write to the magazine for the chart. There is a charge.

Most other countries use the metric system of weights and measures. Yarn weights are indicated in grams. To help you make comparisons, here is a brief conversion table:

1 ounce (oz.)	=	approx. 28.0 grams
1 inch (in.)	=	approx. 2.5 centimeters (cm.)
1 foot (ft.)	=	approx. 30 centimeters
1 meter	=	exactly 100 centimeters
1 yard (yd.)	=	approx. 90 centimeters

Knit and crochet patterns from other countries are also computed in metric, so if you are thinking of knitting a pattern from Italy or Germany or any other country abroad, remember that 2.5(2½) centimeters equal 1 inch. Once I forgot to convert a pattern from metric to our system, and my knitting project turned out large enough to fit 3 people. So watch out!

11

A Question of Sleeves, Armholes, and Shoulders

Soft shaping and unconstructed clothing designs have virtually eliminated the necessity for complicated armhole shaping. Before the relaxed fit was introduced, a major problem was manipulating the sleeve edge to fit the armhole opening perfectly. If all the pieces didn't match exactly, the sleeves stuck up like wings. They looked terrible.

The sleeves, armholes and shoulders described in this book are based on the simple "T" shape, which will fit anyone. The shoulder is dropped slightly, and no special fitting is necessary. A decided advantage is that this design is comfortable and arm movements aren't restricted. A new knitter will be able to make a successful sweater the first time out. Here's how:

First, plan how long you want your sweater to be from shoulder to hem. De-

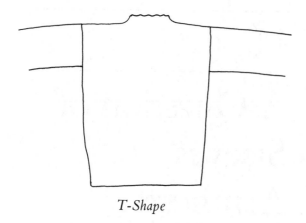

T-Shape

cide how deep an armhole opening will be comfortable for you. If you have a favorite sweater, use it for a guide. So let's pretend that the armhole measurement is 10 inches, plus ¼-inch for the shoulder seam—10¼ inches total. Knit the front and back pieces straight up from the sweater hem. Place a safety pin or yarn marker 10¼ inches below the shoulder, at the edges of each section. With right sides facing, sew the front and back shoulders together. The measurement between the markers, *after sewing,* should be 20 inches. Therefore, the armhole edge of the sleeve should also measure 20 inches.

With a gauge of 4 stitches to the inch, multiplied by 20 inches, there should be 80 stitches when the sleeve is completed.

Open the two sections and lay them out on the table, or any flat surface, and measure the distance between the yarn markers. Are there 20 inches between the markers? Then you're OK.

Plan your sleeve to fit that opening. Check the diagram showing your body measurements. Start with the wrist. Again, this is only a "for instance." If your

wrist measures 8 inches, and the gauge is 4 stitches to the inch, then you would cast on 32 stitches for the cuff. Make the cuff as deep as you want—we'll say 3 inches. For a blousy sleeve, on the next row, increase 1 stitch in *every* stitch (64 stitches and 16 inches wide). You need add only 4 more inches (or 16 stitches) to the width. You have 16 inches above the cuff in which to add the additional stitches. Since each stitch is equal to ¼ inch, you should increase 1 stitch each side every 2 inches, 8 times. This gives you a total of 80 stitches when you've reached a sleeve length of 19 inches, including the cuff. Bind off loosely.

Do you like your sleeves longer? Work *even* after the last increase to the desired length. For a shorter sleeve, add the addi-

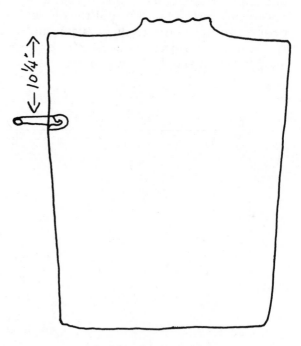

Marking depth of armhole

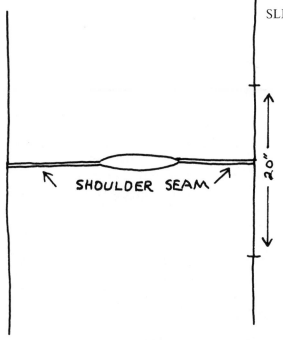

Marking off for sleeve

the seam), or 16 inches at the armhole edge between the markers. The gauge is 4 stitches to the inch. The wrist measurement is 6 inches, and the total length of the sleeve is 18 inches. So, you'll cast on 24 stitches for the cuff. You still need to add 40 more stitches for a 16-inch measurement at the top of the sleeve, and you have 15 inches in which to add those stitches. Increase 1 stitch each side every ¾ inch, until 40 stitches have been added (64 stitches). Fortunately, absolute precision is not crucial with the no-shape armhole and sleeve, so if you are a row or two short of the desired length, work those additional rows even. If you have an extra couple of rows, just push up your sleeve a bit, or fold back the cuff. That's what I do.

The perfectly straight sleeve is easiest of all. First decide the depth of the armhole, and the number of stitches, and work even until the sleeve is whatever length you want. Bind off.

You can knit a sleeve any length you please, as long as the armhole edge of the sleeve fits into the space you've set aside. Since there's no armhole shaping, you won't have to match up curves.

For a puffed or dimpled sleeve, add 2 or 3 inches to the top sleeve width. Pin the top of the sleeve to the armhole, right sides facing. Start pinning at each outside edge toward the center, to within 2 inches each side of the shoulder seam. You'll have a big bunch of material. Ease the remaining material by placing the pins closer together. Try to make the gathers as even as pos-

tional 16 stitches more frequently—about every 1½ inches. Each time you increase 1 stitch at each side, you add ½ inch to the width of the sleeve. Therefore, ½ inch multiplied by 8 will add the additional 4 inches, for a measurement of 20 inches at the armhole edge of the sleeve.

Check the drawings again to be sure you understand how it all works. It's really pretty simple.

What if you want to make a narrower sleeve and armhole? Well, it works the same way. First decide how deep you want the armhole. Let's say this one will be 8 inches deep. Place your markers at that point on the front and back pieces 8¼ inches down from the shoulder (¼ inch for

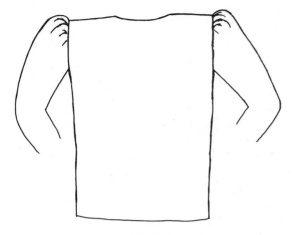

Puffed sleeve

To make a simple gathered sleeve, short or long, just eliminate the ribbed cuff. After all the seams have been sewn, fold the bottom edge of the sleeve to the wrong side about ½ inch, and slip stitch in place with matching yarn. (Slip-stitching is the same as overcasting.) Catch just the loop of the stitch so the stitching won't show on the right side. Measure off a narrow strip of elastic to fit your wrist or arm, and slide it through the hem. Sew the two ends of the elastic together, and that's all there is to it! Instant gathered sleeve.

sible. After all the pins have been positioned, *baste* the sleeve edge to the armhole edge before you sew to prevent the gathers from shifting around.

Even though this sounds like a broken record, it bears repeating—don't go into a tizzy about that extra stitch or two. Knitted material can be wiggled around and be made to fit. Just don't let it scare you.

Don't you hate it when the cuffs of your sweater sleeves stretch out of shape? They look awful. Here's a happy solution that works for me. Weave three or four rows of elastic thread through the inside of the cuff. Use the tapestry needle to do this after all the parts have been connected. From the bottom of the cuff and at the seam edge, weave the elastic thread through the back loop of every second or third stitch, around back to the seam. Draw the elastic in until your hand slides in and out easily. Work the needle over the last stitch a couple of times to fasten it firmly. When you push up the sleeves, the cuffs will stay in place. Sneaky, huh?

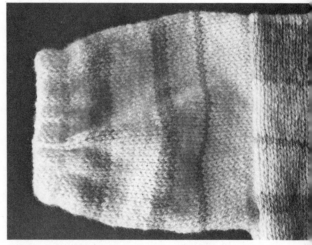

Gathered sleeve (detail)

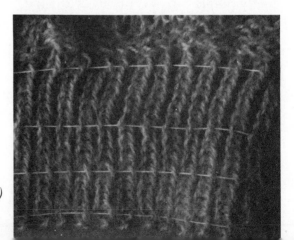

Elastic thread (detail)

12

Make It Personal

Personalize your sweaters with interesting details. Add a collar or a pocket to a basic design, and your sweater is instantly transformed. How about a ruffle around the neckline, around the cuff, or somewhere along the sleeve? Use your own combinations of easy pattern stitches (they don't have to be complicated), or colors, or combinations of yarns for that special touch. Crochet the parts together on the right side with a contrasting or blending color. Use a different color for each part of the sweater. Make a reversible, sleeveless jacket.

Worn-out lace tablecloths need not be thrown away. Make a lace collar to wear over your basic pullover. Use a blouse collar for a guide.

Ideas are just waiting to be invented—so start inventing.

For example. Your sweater is a simple, sleeveless, straight-line pullover, with a bateau (boatline) neckline. Nothing fancy. But you've worn the sweater a million times. You still love it, but want to jazz it up. How about adding sleeves (page 53), perhaps in a new color? Knit the sleeves in garter stitch or stockinette stitch, or one of the easy pattern stitches described on pages 45–48. With another color, trim the armholes and the neckline with a row of single crochet. Add a row of crochet around the bottom of the sweater, too. Knit a pocket from the contrasting color, and sew it on one of the sleeves. Knit two patch pockets and sew them somewhere else.

Sewing on collar

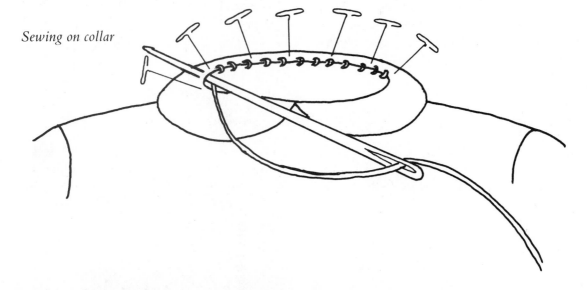

13

Ruffles

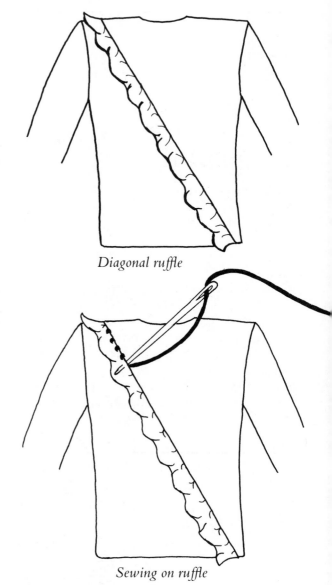

Diagonal ruffle

Sewing on ruffle

Does your sweater already have sleeves? How about ruffling them? Add a ruffle down one side of your sweater, or diagonally from shoulder to hem. To avoid laundering or cleaning problems, be sure to make the ruffle from the same type of yarn. Here's how:

Measure the length from shoulder seam to hem, or just above the ribbing, if you prefer. With the same size needle as used for the sweater (if you can remember) knit a sample stitch gauge. Multiply the gauge by the number of inches from shoulder to hem. With a gauge of 4 stitches to the inch and a measurement of 16 inches, cast on 64 stitches. Knit one row. On the next row, increase 1 stitch in *every* stitch (128 stitches). Work even for 1½ or 2 inches, or to desired depth of ruffle, in garter, stockinette, or seed stitch for added texture. Bind off.

Attaching a Ruffle

Lay the sweater on a flat, padded surface. Your ironing board is just fine. Do you want the ruffle on the left or right side of the sweater? For a right-side ruffle, the wide edge should face the right seam. Reverse it for opposite side. Place the ruffle on the sweater from shoulder to hem. Pin one short edge to the shoulder

Neckline, sleeve and bottom ruffles

Vertical ruffle

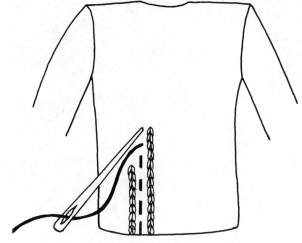

Marking for vertical ruffle

seam; pin the other short edge to the bottom of the sweater, or just above the ribbing. Pin along the narrow edge, easing in along the way, if necessary. Before you start to pin the edge, thread a tapestry nee-

dle with a contrasting color and run through a straight vertical line of stitches from shoulder to hem. This will assist you in keeping the ruffle in a straight line. Then pin the edge.

Thread the tapestry needle with matching yarn and neatly overcast the narrow edge to the sweater. Watch it—don't stitch the front to the back of the sweater. Pull the loose ends to the inside and weave them in. (page 72)

Add a ruffle around one or both armholes, around the top of the ribbed cuffs, or around the neckline—or anywhere else you please, now that you know how to make them.

Ruffled neckline

14

Pockets

Pockets can be decorative as well as functional. Almost everything I knit has a pocket somewhere. Pockets provide a resting place for my hands when I don't know what else to do with them; for carrying a Kleenex; and they are a good way to add surface interest.

You can put a pocket anywhere you want to—in the usual place, on the sleeves, near a shoulder, or a great big pocket across the front of your sweater. Pockets may be knitted right into the material—these are called "insert" pockets. Knit separate pockets and sew them on—"patch" pockets. Patch pockets allow you some design freedom because it isn't necessary to plan ahead. Make them from the same or contrasting color, or even a completely different stitch. Attach them with matching or contrasting yarn. Crochet one row of single crochet all around the edge, then stitch them to the sweater.

The insert pocket is knitted directly into the material so it's necessary to decide before you start your sweater where to place it.

One of my favorite pockets is the sweatshirt, or "kangaroo" pocket. It adds spark to the surface design, provides a place to keep keys, etc., and will keep your hands warm, too.

Patch Pockets

We'll do the patch pocket first. After looking carefully at your sweater, you've decided to add the pocket just above the ribbing. For a stitch gauge of 5 stitches to the inch, and width of 20 inches, a 20-stitch (or 4-inch wide) pocket is ample. Cast on 20 stitches and work even in garter, stockinette, or ribbing (if the contrast looks interesting), for 4 or 5 inches, or whatever depth appeals to you. Some instruction books recommend that pockets be placed an exact number of inches up from the hem and an exact number of inches in from the side seam. About 3 inches in from the side edge seems to work, but it's your sweater, so you can put them anywhere you want to.

This may seem a bit nutty to you, but here's how I decide where to place the front pockets on my sweaters. Hold your arms close to your body, with the elbows bent at right angles. Let your hands flop down, just like a begging dog. Your fingertips will fall at just about the right spot for a comfortable pocket. Do you feel silly? (If anybody's watching tell them you're relaxing your fingers.) Make a note of the number of inches from the bottom of the sweater to the top of the pocket, and place a T-pin or a marker at that spot. If 3 inches in from the side edge seems about right, place another pin there. Place a pin at each of the four corners, then a couple more between each of the pins. Overcast three sides, leaving the top open. Make the over-

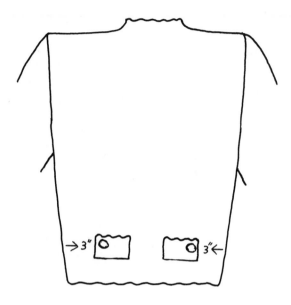

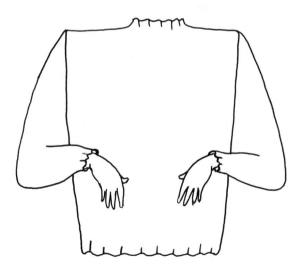

Positioning patch pockets

cast stitches as neat and close together as possible.

Patch pockets may also be sewn on sideways or even angled, or any other way you invent. Use the side edges of the sweater and the top of the ribbed hem as guides. Don't forget to leave one side unstitched! Before stitching any of the pockets to the sweater, add that row of single crochet all around the edge. The pocket will be easier to pin and sew.

Most of the sweaters in this book were designed to be switched from front to back, so pockets on both sides could add yet another detail. You're the wearer, so these kinds of decisions are up to you.

Insert Pocket

Insert pockets are neat and unobtrusive, but they are more complex than patch pockets. For now you can skip this chapter if you want to, and come back to it another time after you've accumulated more experience. There's no sense in cluttering up your mind with more difficult techniques until you're ready for them. Remember that the information is here when you feel like trying.

Insert pocket linings should be knitted ahead of time, so you'll need to decide the depth and width of the pocket before starting the sweater front. For this experiment cast on 20 stitches and knit even in stockinette stitch for 3 inches. That's depth of the pocket. Leave a 3-inch end and cut the yarn. Slip these stitches onto a holder and put them aside. No matter what stitch you

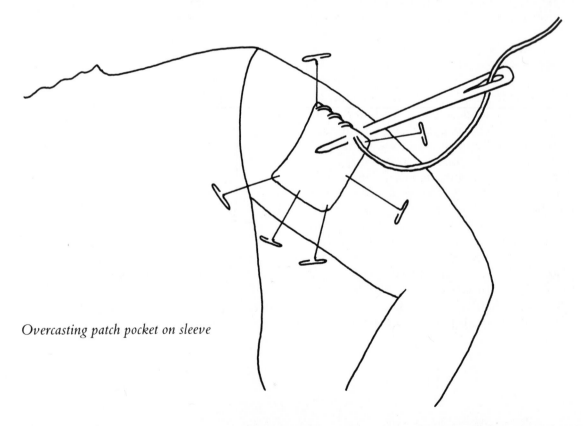

Overcasting patch pocket on sleeve

Right side—insert pocket

Insert pocket lining

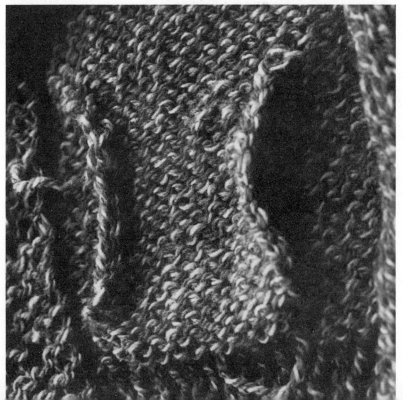

use for the main parts of the sweater, make the pocket linings from stockinette stitch. They're less bulky.

Now we'll go back to the 30-stitch practice swatch. On the right side facing you, knit the first 5 stitches and bind off the next 20 stitches. The number of bound-off stitches should match the width of the linings made earlier. To bind off in the middle of a row, after knitting the first 5 stitches, knit 2 more stitches. Pull the second stitch on the right needle over the first stitch on that needle (Binding Off, page 23). Continue binding off until there are 4 stitches on the left needle and one stitch on the right needle, after the bound-off stitches. Knit the remaining stitches. On the next row, work the first 5 stitches. Knit the 20 stitches of the insert from the holder (if you

Pinning insert pocket lining

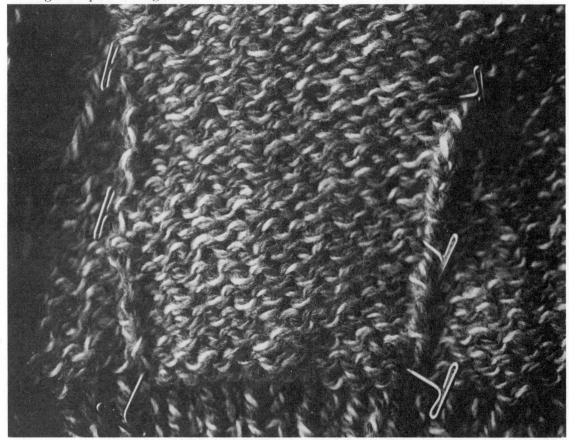

are on a purl row, you should purl the stitches from the holder), and complete the row.

Continue knitting. The pocket lining has been inserted directly into your sweater. Isn't that neat? Practice knitting a couple of insert pockets before working them into a sweater.

After completing this section of the sweater, but *before* sewing the side seams, turn your work to the wrong side and carefully pin, then baste the pocket flap to the material, before sewing it in permanently. Carefully slipstitch the flap. Be sure to catch only the back loop. Weave in any loose threads at each side of the pocket.

This is another time when perhaps someone else should read these directions aloud as you work with the needles and yarn.

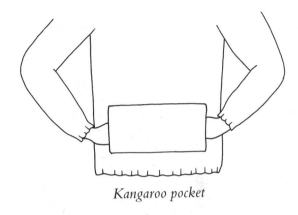

Kangaroo pocket

Sweat Shirt (Kangaroo) Pocket

The sweat shirt (kangaroo) pocket, or stomacher as I call it, is one of my favorites. This is an exaggerated version of a patch pocket. It's both practical and decorative. This pocket should be at least 8 inches wide and 7 inches deep. Have you a favorite sweat shirt with a pocket? Use that as an example.

Cast on 50 stitches. At the *beginning* and *end* of every row, work 6 stitches in garter stitch, and the 38 in-between in stockinette stitch. The 6 stitches at each edge form a neat, flat vertical border. Work this way for about 7 inches, ending on the wrong side. Bind off all the stitches.

Attaching the Sweat Shirt Pocket

Lay the knitted rectangle on the sweater front, just above the ribbing (if any), or about 2 inches from the bottom of the sweater. Carefully center the pocket so that the short side edges are an equal distance from each side seam edge. Pin each of the four corners, then pin the top and bottom edges. Place the T-pins at right angles to the material. Leave the side edges free. Thread your tapestry needle with matching yarn and neatly overcast the bottom and top edges. Pull the loose ends through to the wrong side and weave them in. (Chapter 16)

Knit the pocket from the same color yarn as the body of the sweater, or make it a contrasting color. When you are bored with one color, remove the overcast

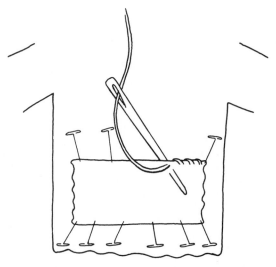

Pinning and sewing kangaroo pocket

15

Connections

stitches and knit a new pocket from another color. Tie the whole design together with a touch of the new color somewhere else on the sweater—around the armhole, down the side seams, or anywhere else. The extra touch of color will give a pulled-together, professional appearance, rather than looking like an afterthought.

No matter how even the knitted stitches, or how perfectly all the pieces match, the true mark of a carefully done sweater, with a look of professionalism, is how neatly each section is connected to the other.

Putting all the pieces together can be a bear for even the most experienced. I know many knitters who are willing to pay someone else to do it for them because they've never learned how to properly connect the parts.

Fledgling knitters, just testing their knitting wings, often balk at the job. But believe me when I say that a neatly done seam will make the difference between a tacky looking, home-made garment, and a handmade you can take pride in.

So, the finishing is as important as the knitting. If you will accept this as a part of the whole knitting experience (as I keep repeating), then connecting the parts neatly will become as automatic as the knitting. As you begin to understand the principle of assembling, any mistakes you may have overlooked can easily be hidden, one way or another.

Experience is a great teacher, so don't expect that first seam to be perfect. But you don't have to be a sewing whiz, either. It took me a while before I felt happy with the appearance of my seams.

There are several ways to connect the seams of a hand knit; backstitch, crochet, overcast, and woven. There are also differences of opinion about which is most desirable. Personally, I prefer either the backstitch or the crocheted seam, and only occasionally the overcast method. The backstitch is my first choice. It looks professional, and it's strong at the stress points, such as shoulders, sleeves, necklines, and sides. Also, it allows you to make alterations, if necessary. If your sweater is a bit too large, make a regular seam with a seam allowance, just as though you were sewing woven material—unless, of course, the yarn is fat and bulky. Then it's better to crochet the seam, or backstitch with a finer yarn.

I mentioned the woven seam, but I never use it. It does make a flat seam, but has no strength. (The stitching eventually begins to separate.) Unless the edges are perfectly matched, it can be pretty unsightly. So I'm going to ignore it in this book.

Overcast seams, in my opinion, are not sturdy enough to take much stress. After a few wearings they, too, begin to separate and look rather messy. However, overcasting (slip-stitching) is acceptable for sewing on pockets and other surface details.

You'll learn how to backstitch and crochet seams, and when to appropriately overcast. To begin, lay out all the parts on a flat surface. Do the front and back match? How about the sleeves? Are they the same length and width? Check these points before you connect them. Are you satisfied that everything is OK?

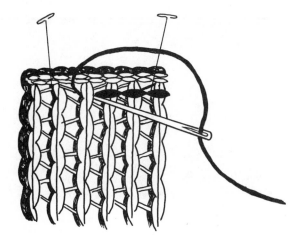

Backstitching seam

Pin, then baste, all the parts together (use plenty of pins). Try on your sweater. Does it fit in all the right places? Then you are ready for the final sewing. The parts should be sewn with your tapestry needle and matching yarn in this order:

First the shoulder seams, then the sleeve and side seams. (Collars or decorations may be added later.) Here's how: With the right sides together, measure off an opening large enough to fit over your head (about 8 inches should be enough), and backstitch the front and back shoulders together. The stitch tension should be as flexible as the tension of the knitted material. Should the backstitching be too tight, the seam may pop and you'll have to redo the whole seam. So be on your guard!

Detail—backstitching seam

Backstitch Seam

Start at the right shoulder edge, as close to the bound-off stitches as possible. Leaving a short length of yarn (do *not* tie a knot), work from right to left and put the threaded tapestry needle through both pieces from underneath about ¼ inch from the edge. Go back over the edge and up through both pieces about ¼ inch to the left of the first stitch. Then put the needle, from *front to back*, back into the material right up against that first stitch. Come up from the back again about ¼ inch to the left of the last sewn stitch. Continue this way until you reach the opposite edge. Work the needle in and out of the last stitch once more, and over the left edge. Leave a short length of yarn and cut it.

After sewing the shoulder seams, fold the armhole edge of the sleeve in half, right sides facing. Place a T-pin at the center of the fold. Use the center pin as a guide, then measure the distance from the pin to one outer edge. With right sides of body and sleeve facing, pin the sleeve to the armhole at that point. Pin the opposite side the same way. The distance between the center pin and each side should be the same. Use plenty of pins to connect the remaining edges. The other sleeve should be pinned to the armhole the same way. Hold one armhole edge up to the other. Are they the same? If not, adjust the pins and material so they match.

Backstitch each armhole seam immediately *underneath* the bound-off sleeve stitches, sewing from right to left. Sewing underneath the bound-off stitches helps to prevent those bound-off loops from sneaking through to the right side. Loose edge stitches can be hidden at the same time.

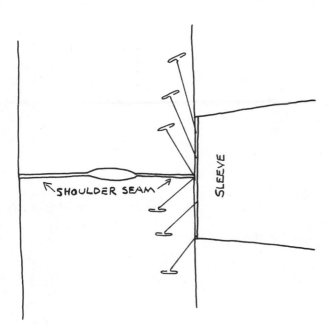

Attaching sleeve

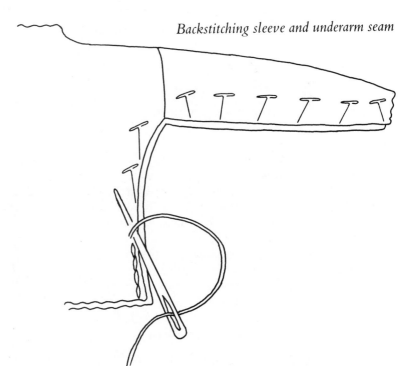

Backstitching sleeve and underarm seam

Pin the underarm and side edges together. Start at the cuff or sweater hem (either end is OK), pin all the way down the length of the sleeve and continue down the side of the sweater. There will be one long underarm seam from cuff to hem. This is less complicated than sewing the side and sleeve seams first, and then trying to fit the sleeve into the armhole. A lot less bulky, too. Should you want to make the sweater wider or narrower, if, or when, your measurements change, there's just one continuous seam to undo.

Firmly fasten the last stitch, snip the yarn. Sew the other seam the same way. Weave in the loose ends.

Crochet Seam

A crocheted seam is bulkier than the backstitch. I recommend this method only if the additional bulk will not distort the fit, or it is intentionally used to decorate. On the positive side, a crocheted seam is easy to unravel. Undo the last stitch and with one yank, the whole seam is opened. There are two methods—slip-stitch crochet and single crochet.

The *single crocheted seam* has a definite ridge riding on top of the joined edges. The *slip-stitch crocheted* seam is flatter, but less flexible. Because it is less flexible, you should be especially alert to maintain the same tension as your knitting. Try both on a sample first.

SLIP-STITCH CROCHETED SEAM

Step 1: Pin the two edges together.

Step 2: Start at the right edge, with right sides facing, leave a 3- or 4-inch length of yarn, and put the crochet hook through both pieces.

Step 3: Catch the working yarn with the hook and pull it through the stitches of both edges at the same time. There is one loop on the hook.

Step 4: Put the hook through the next stitches of both pieces, catch the yarn and pull it through the material and through the loop on the hook at the same time. There is still one loop on the hook.

Continue in this manner along the edge until the whole seam is completed. To fasten off the seam, snip the yarn and firmly pull the cut end through the last loop on the hook.

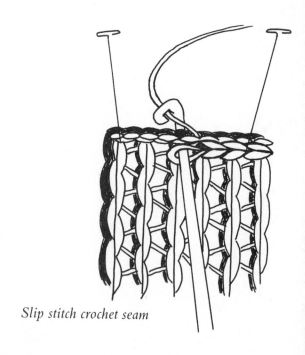

Slip stitch crochet seam

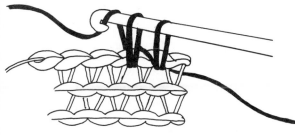

Single crochet seam

of the original yarn will mask the substitute, and the difference will never be noticeable. Another plus—needlepoint yarns may be purchased in very small amounts.

SINGLE CROCHETED SEAM

Repeat steps 1, 2 and 3 of slip-stitch crochet.

Step 4: Put the hook through the next stitches and pull the yarn through the material. There are 2 loops on the hook.
Step 5: Catch the yarn again and pull it through both loops. You have made one single crocheted join.

First pin, then baste all the parts together before starting to crochet the seams. This is especially important if the seam will be visible on the right side of the sweater. You'll have better control. Crochet the stitches as evenly spaced as you can. Your sweater will look much nicer.

Connect the seams with the same yarn as that used for the sweater whenever possible. If the yarn is too fat, or has lots of bumps, try to find a flat yarn in the same (or blending) color and fiber content. I often use needlepoint wool, which is ideal for sewing up. It is available in several weights, and it's strong. You'll find every color imaginable, so surely you'll be able to find something suitable. The thickness

Single crochet seam—detail

Overcasting Seams

With right sides facing, position the two parts to be connected next to each other. Place the T-pins crosswise on the two edges. With your tapestry needle threaded with matching (or contrasting) yarn—depending on the design—working from right to left, put the needle through the edge stitch of both parts, and anchor it. Put the needle through both parts again, from back to front, and over the top of the edge. Make another stitch. Continue this way to the opposite edge. Try to keep the overcast stitches as even as possible, and don't pull them too firmly, to avoid puckering. Go over the last stitch one more time, and fasten off.

Whichever method you choose for connecting all the sections, make a real attempt to match up the pieces. If the design includes stripes, be sure that the stripes meet neatly at the seams.

These are a few choices to consider when it's time to put everything together. The rest is all up to you. You're the boss.

16

Loose Ends

Those loose ends left dangling after you've sewn the seams or joined in a new ball of yarn, or added the pockets, should be worked back into the material. NEVER CUT THEM! Why? Because you'll have a neater sweater, and the cut ends won't work loose. Grab the crochet hook and I'll tell you how.

At the seams, slide the crochet hook through the top stitch of the seam, catch

Overcasting seam

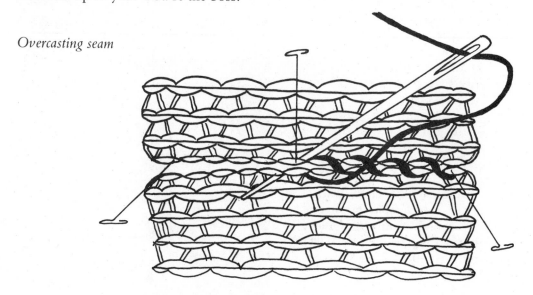

Weaving in loose ends

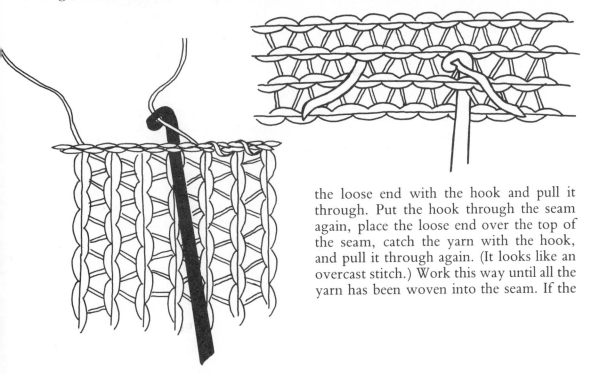

the loose end with the hook and pull it through. Put the hook through the seam again, place the loose end over the top of the seam, catch the yarn with the hook, and pull it through again. (It looks like an overcast stitch.) Work this way until all the yarn has been woven into the seam. If the

17
One into Many

loose end is very long (more than 6 or 7 inches), weave it in anyway. This is a security blanket because you may just need those few extra inches in case you want to unravel the sweater some other time. I never waste even an inch for just that reason.

Did you join a new ball of yarn in the body of your sweater? Those loose ends should be woven in, too. Turn the sweater wrong side out. Notice that the two ends fall in the opposite direction from the knitting. With your crochet hook, pull one of the ends through a loop just below the connection, and continue this through every other loop until there's just a smidgen of yarn left. Leave it. Work the other end the same way. Should the end work itself through to the right side, pull it back through with your hook.

Knitters don't like to monkey around with loose ends either. It's scut work and tedious, so save this job for when you're listening to the stereo or watching television. It will go much faster. Neatness counts here, too. Even if this part of knitting doesn't sound like much fun, it will make a whale of a difference in the appearance of your sweater.

Many different sweater designs from one basic pattern? Of course, and probably more than are suggested here, when you put your thinking cap on. Make a smashing original from a basic pullover with a touch of surface decoration anywhere you like. Use two colors—one for the back and another for the front. Alternate sleeve colors, too. Insert a simple pattern stitch, or make the front from stockinette stitch and the back from garter stitch. Where does it say you can't? This is designing.

Tread the design waters cautiously. Make that first experience a pleasure instead of a pain. Here are the directions for a go-with-everything pullover. Wear it with or without a blouse—with jeans, shorts, or a skirt. The main stitch is garter stitch, with ribbed cuffs and hem. The yarn is pure wool, machine-washable knitting worsted. What could be more practical and inexpensive?

The directions for the sweater are calculated to fit a 32-inch bust. If that's you, go ahead and follow them as they are written. If your bust size is *smaller* or *fuller,* then read Chapter 5 again. It tells you how to take your measurements. Read the chapter on gauge, too. You'll easily be able to make the adjustments to fit you.

Author wearing basic pullover, body and sleeves all garter stitched, ribbed cuffs and hem.

The same pullover with fringes added

Go-With-Everything Pullover:

Size: Directions are for size 32 bust. Width of back or front at underarms—17 inches. Length—shoulder to hem—18 inches or desired length. Sleeve length—18 inches finished.

Materials: 3 4-oz. skeins or balls wool knitting worsted (plus one extra for good measure).

Knitting needles—1 pair each 8 and 10, or size to obtain gauge

Tapestry needle with blunt point

Crochet hook

Tape measure

Scissors

T-pins

Gauge: 4 stitches = 1 inch

Back and *front* are the same. Start at lower edge with # 8 needles, cast on 68 stitches. Work in knit 1, purl 1 ribbing for 3 inches. Change to # 10 needles, increase 1 stitch at beginning and end of next row (70 stitches). Work even in garter stitch until work measures 18 inches or desired length. Bind off loosely.

Front: Same as back.

Sleeves: Make two. With smaller needles, cast on 24 stitches. Work in knit 1, purl 1 ribbing for 3 inches. Change to larger needle. On the next row, work in garter stitch, and increase 1 stitch at beginning and end of the row. Continue in garter stitch, increasing 1 stitch each side every inch, 14 more times (54 stitches, or 18 inches wide). The sleeve length above the 3-inch ribbing should measure 15 inches, or a total of 18 inches. Bind off loosely.

Connect all the pieces as described on pages 66–72.

This photo shows another version of that same basic sweater with a couple of exceptions—the front and back are each different colors of wool knitting worsted—in this case white and purple were used. One sleeve is white and one purple. The sweater parts are connected with single crochet on the right side with the white yarn. Wear this sweater either way—front and back are the same.

The third adaptation of the same sweater is shown also. This time instead of plain garter stitch, squares of garter stitch were alternated with seed stitch squares in the body of the sweater and the sleeves. Instead of gradually increasing the width of the sleeves, the increasing was done on the first row above the ribbed cuff.

Are you getting the idea? The pattern squares measure about 8½ inches across and about 7½ inches deep in this particular version. Yours don't have to be exactly the same. You can make them any width and depth you like.

Gigi shows two sides of basic pullover, with matching hat.

The back and front pieces are exactly the same. Decide the number of stitches corresponding to the stitch gauge and your own measurements. Divide that number in half. With the smaller needle, work in knit 1, purl 1 ribbing for 3 inches. Change to larger needles and work half the stitches on the needle in *seed stitch*. Place a marker at that point. Work the remaining stitches in *garter stitch*. Continue working even, but remember to change stitch patterns after the marker. When your work measures 7½ inches (or whatever depth you prefer) leave the marker in place, alternate the pattern stitches, and make this set of pattern blocks the same way. Change to smaller needles and work the last 2 inches in knit 1, purl 1 ribbing. Bind off. There's no right or wrong side to this pattern. Both are the same. Wear it either way. Backstitch all the parts together (Chapter 15). This time be sure that the pattern blocks meet at the side seams.

Sleeves: Make two. With smaller needle, cast on 24 stitches and work 3 inches (or desired length) in knit 1, purl 1, ribbing. On next row, increase 1 stitch in every stitch along the row (48 stitches). Working in first pattern block, increase 1 stitch at beginning and end of a row every 4 inches, 3 times. At the same time, change to second block when sleeve above ribbing measures 8 or 8½ inches. Finish sleeve. Bind off in pattern.

Still another design from that original pullover sweater: eliminate the ribbing, and knit all the parts in straight garter stitch. For a lacier look, use a larger needle

Dana models front and back of pullover combining alternating squares of seed stitch and garter stitch with poufed sleeves and single ribbed hem, cuffs and neckline.

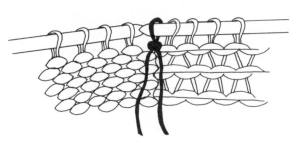

Yarn marker between squares

Detail—seed stitch and garter stitch squares combined

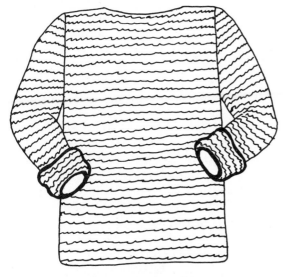

Rolled back cuff

—perhaps a #13. Find your gauge—mine was 2½ stitches to the inch. If your knitting is looser or tighter, be sure to do your arithmetic before you start. The stitch gauge will change, and the sweater measurements will change in length and width. Wear it over a turtleneck and belt it in at the waist. Flip the sleeves back, and bingo! instant cuffs. Get the idea?

Convert the original sweater into a vest. Omit the sleeves. Knit the back as usual. For one side of vest front, cast on 32

stitches, plus 3 more stitches (1 inch), or the appropriate number. With another ball of yarn, cast on the same number of stitches for the second side of front. Work even on both pieces at the same time, dropping first ball of yarn and picking up second ball of yarn. Knit the desired length. Bind off each side.

Here is the basic sweater as a sleeveless pullover. The sleeves were omitted, and a braided drawstring was woven through the top of the ribbing. Two 4-oz. skeins of wool knitting worsted should be ample. Do you have some yarn left over? Make a matching hat. Or stash it away. Perhaps you'll want to add sleeves some day.

By now you've had enough experience to try working with a more glamorous yarn, perhaps a mohair, or a thick and thin. Select a textured yarn that feels good to the touch. Keep in mind, before you jump in, that highly-textured or long-haired yarn must be closely watched because the stitches are harder to recognize.

You'll probably be attracted to the beautiful mohair yarns, and I don't blame you. They are luscious, but tricky, especially for beginners. The long hairs of the yarn tend to stick together. Should you need to unravel, each stitch must be carefully picked apart, and sometimes you'll be fighting with them.

Knitting two parts at same time

Basic pullover with bateau neckline and short sleeves

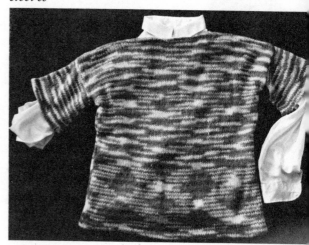

However, you should try some of the textured yarns. Look for yarn sales and buy one ball for practice.

The big shirt sweater on page 83 was made from a short-haired combination mohair and wool. There was only enough of the main color to knit most of the sweater, but not enough to complete it. I was lucky to find some odd balls of the same yarn in other colors, so I added stripes and bands of ruffles, with enough left over for a cap and a headband.

The sweater can be worn front to back, and can be made from only one color, if you prefer. Make it longer, and you've converted the big shirt into a dress. Wear it over pants, with tights or even a skirt. Wear it with or without a belt. These are a

The sleeveless pullover works just as well for an adult figure.

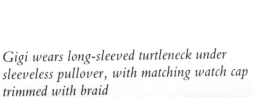

Gigi wears long-sleeved turtleneck under sleeveless pullover, with matching watch cap trimmed with braid

Gigi models garter stitch sleeveless pullover, with drawstring

few of the options open to you. After selecting the yarn, be sure to knit up one ball to determine the amount needed for the whole garment (see page 51). Here are the directions:

Mohair/Wool Big Shirt:

Sizes: One size fits all.
Measurements:
    Width at underarm: 22 inches
    Shoulder to hem: 26 inches
    Underarm to hem: 17 inches
    Sleeve length: 21 inches, including cuff
Gauge: 2½ stitches = 1 inch #13 needle
    3 stitches = 1 inch # 11 needle
Materials: Main color, A: 4 or 5 2-oz. balls
    Mohair/wool, 1 each of other 3 colors B,C,D.
    #11 and #13 needles (or size to obtain gauge)
    Tapestry needle
    Crochet hook
    Tape measure
    Scissors
    Row counter

Back and Front (the same):
With #11 needles, cast on 54 stitches. With main color A, work knit 1, purl 1 ribbing for 2 inches. Change to # 13 needles and work even in stockinette stitch for 15 more inches, or desired length. Change to Color B, work 8 rows even in stockinette stitch, 4 rows color C, 8 rows color D, 2 rows color B. Change back to

main color A and work knit 1, purl 1 ribbing for 2 more inches, ending on wrong side. On next row, bind off 18 stitches for shoulder; complete the row. At beginning of next row, bind off 18 stitches. There are 18 stitches remaining on the needle. Change back to #11 needles and work in knit 1, purl 1 ribbing for 1½ inches. Bind off loosely in pattern. Make the second section (front) exactly the same.

Sleeves: With smaller needle cast on 28 stitches. Work in knit 1, purl 1 ribbing for 2 inches. Change to larger needles, and working in stockinette stitch, increase 1 stitch at beginning and end of next row. Continue in stockinette stitch, increasing 1 stitch at beginning and end of row every 2 inches, 7 more times. At the same time, when work measures about 11 inches, start color bands: with 4 rows color C, 6 rows color B, 4 rows color D, 2 rows color C. Change to main color A and work 2 more inches, or desired length. Bind off.

Ruffles: With smaller needle and appropriate color, pick up stitches across top of each stripe (see page 39). Work 8 rows garter stitch. Bind off.

Sewing up: With right sides facing, pin front and back shoulders together, including extended neck ribbing. Backstitch (page 68) with main color. Pin and sew sleeves to armhole (page 69). Pin and sew sleeve and underarm edges.

Blocking: Turn to wrong side. Dampen cloth and lay over seams. Lightly steam just above material, flattening seams with palm of hand. Turn sweater to right side and allow to dry thoroughly.

The ruffles and stripes in this sweater are optional. If ruffles and stripes aren't your cup of tea, make the whole sweater one color. These decorations can always be

Dana shows front and back of mohair/wool big shirt, with matching rolled brim cap. Yarn courtesy of Tinctoria.

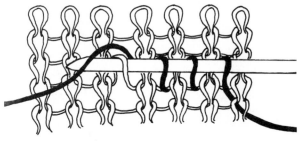

Picking up stitches on surface

added later, if you change your mind. I thought they added a bit of fun. If you decide not to make the ruffles or add the stripes, you'll need a ball or two more of the main color.

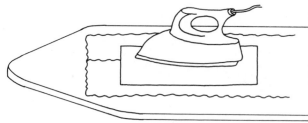

Pressing seam

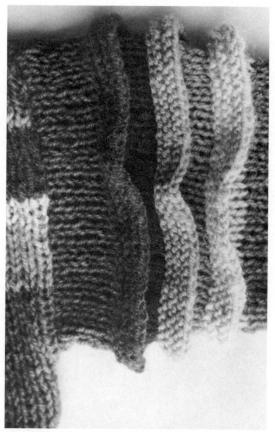

Sleeve ruffles—detail

Rolled Brim Cap

Materials: #10 needles, leftover yarn from Big Shirt.

Gauge: 3½ stitches = 1 inch

Cast on 70 stitches. Work 4 inches even in garter stitch. Change color (optional), and on next row begin stockinette stitch. Work even for 1½ inches, or 8 rows. On next row, change color (optional) and decrease 1 stitch at beginning and end of row. Work 4 rows of new color, then 4 rows of next color. At same time, decrease 1 stitch at beginning and end of every 4th row, 3 more times (62 stitches). Change to main color and decrease 8 stitches evenly spaced on next knit row (54 stitches). Knit or purl 2 together on *every* row until no stitches remain. Fasten off. Sew back seam, carefully matching stripes. No blocking required. Roll up the bottom edge.

Headband

Materials: 2 medium-size, double-pointed needles.

Leftover yarn.

Cast on 5 stitches. In garter stitch, work across row. Don't turn your work. With yarn behind, slide the stitches back to opposite end of double-pointed needle. Knit them again. Work this way until the band is long enough to fit around your head, plus another 6 or 8 inches for the ties. Add the other colors when and where you wish. No blocking required.

Pulling the yarn across the back of the stitches to start the next row leaves a long strand spanning the stitches, and automatically pulls them together. As the cord becomes longer, notice that the back strands resemble the steps on a ladder.

Before you start the headband, practice this technique to understand how it works.

This technique is also useful for making lacings and narrow cords. Try it with only 3 stitches, or any number of stitches, just to see what happens.

If you've made all three parts, you have a coordinated group of knits, which may be worn together or paired with other garments in your closet. Choose the yarns and colors that suit you.

The freedom of choice, combined with common sense and a spirit of adventure, should give your self-confidence a boost. Certainly it will enhance your knitting awareness. Go for it!

Headband

18

Buttons and Buttonholes

The time will come when you will want to make a cardigan sweater or a jacket. As long as you're learning how to knit, learn to make buttonholes, too. The horizontal and eyelet buttonholes are the simplest to make. The placement should be determined before starting your sweater.

Make a note of the center front length, from center neckline to the bottom of the sweater, then decide the size of the buttonhole. Some knitters choose the buttons when they buy the yarn. Some choose after the sweater is sewn together. It really makes no difference. It is important that the button fit the buttonhole and that the buttonholes are spaced evenly, without gapping. For a sweater knitted from fat, bulky yarn, about 4½ inches apart is pretty average. For medium or knitting worsted weight yarns, 3 to 4 inches apart is a good rule to follow. On a basic cardigan, plan the first buttonhole about 1 inch below the collarline, and the last about the same from the bottom of the sweater.

Markers for placement of buttons

For example: the measurement from the neckline to the bottom of the sweater is 18 inches. Less the inch at the top and bottom, there are 16 inches to work with. Divide 16 by 3 and this tells you that you need to make 5 buttonholes about 3 or 3⅛ inches apart.

Horizontal Buttonhole

Let's assume you are knitting a sweater for yourself. The buttonhole will be on the right side of the garment (left side facing you). (On a real sweater, for accuracy, knit both sides at the same time with two separate balls of yarn.) Starting with the right section facing you, work to within 6 stitches from the end (3 stitch buttonhole and 3 stitch front border). Attach a marker of contrasting yarn and leave it there. This will tell you exactly where to sew on the button. Finish the row. Drop the yarn. Pick up the second ball of yarn, knit 3 stitches, knit the next two stitches and pull the first stitch over the second. Do this twice more. You've bound off 3 stitches.

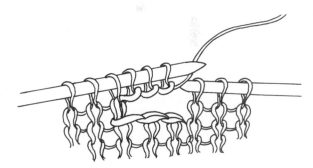

Binding off for buttonhole

Complete the row. On the next row, work to within 1 stitch before the bound-off stitches of the row below. Increase 1 stitch in that stitch, and cast on 2 stitches. Com-

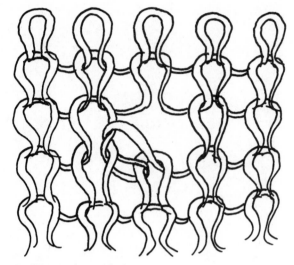

Bull's-eye buttonhole

plete the row. When working the second buttonhole row, always increase 1 stitch before the bound-off section, and cast on 1 stitch less than the number of bound-off stitches on the row below. Two rows of knitting are required to make a bound-off horizontal buttonhole. On the first row the necessary number of stitches to fit the button are bound off. On the second row, the same number of stitches are added back on, directly over the bound-off stitches of the preceding row.

Ordinarily you would cast on the *same* number of stitches over the bound-off stitches. However, the cast-on stitches are looser than the bound-off stitches, and often leave an unsightly loose stitch at the inner corner. It's not neat.

However, by *increasing* one stitch in the stitch immediately before the bound-off stitches of the previous row, and *casting* on only 2 stitches, that loose corner stitch can be avoided.

Neatly overcast the buttonhole with matching yarn. If the working yarn is too fat or too bumpy, try to find a matching or blending yarn in a finer weight.

Bull's-Eye Buttonhole

I call this a bull's-eye buttonhole because it's just a big hole made with a yarn-over. It's the easiest to make and doesn't require reinforcement with additional stitching.

Again, work to within 4 stitches of the edge and place the colored yarn marker there. On the opposite section, with the second ball of yarn, knit 4 stitches, yarn over, knit 2 together and finish the row. On the next row, work the yarn-over as a regular stitch. Nothing to it.

Practice making both types of buttonholes before you start your sweater. Don't forget to record any comments in your notebook.

Buttons

Select the buttons carefully for that very special hand knit. Be sure the button slides into the buttonhole easily without pulling at the fabric. You'll have a hard time choosing, because, like yarns, there are a million different kinds. Sometimes an unusual button will be all the decoration you need. It can make a difference. Use cotton thread in a matching color to sew the button to your sweater. Yarn isn't satisfactory because it soon will begin to stretch, and the button will be left flopping around. If your sweater has been knitted with big needles, a little patch of cotton material held to the wrong side and stitched along with the button will hold the button firmly in place.

Buttons are an inexpensive and colorful way to decorate your knits.

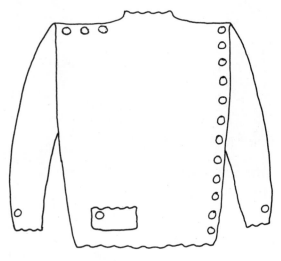

Buttons as decoration

19

Lightning Strips

One of the handiest tricks to add to your knitting know-how is bias knitting, or lightning strips, as I call them. Bias strips are useful for trimming sweater edges, pockets, and necklines, or for just sewing onto the surface of your sweater. Garter or stockinette stitch are used most frequently for bias knitting. Bias strips may be knitted with any number of stitches. Slant the bias to the left or to the right, or in both directions on the same strip. Make them wide or narrow. Here's how:

Left Bias

With any size needles and your practice yarn, cast on 10 stitches. Knit one row. On the next row, knit the first 2 stitches together, work across and *increase* 1 stitch in the last stitch. Turn your work and knit even for one row. On the next row, again knit 2 together and increase 1 stitch in the last stitch. You always work with the same number of stitches. Decreasing at the *beginning* of the row and increasing at the *end* will slope the material to the left.

Lightning strip (detail)

Gigi shows lightning strip decoration

Right Bias

Leave those stitches on the needle and start the right bias by *increasing* 1 stitch in the first stitch and *decreasing* 1 stitch at the end of the row. Work this way on *every other* row until you can see the right slope of the stitches. Now change back to the left bias.

Bind off on the even row. The edges will be jagged, and because colors may be added at any time, bias knitting offers many decorative and finishing possibilities. Fool around with bias knitting, and then use it to decorate or trim a special sweater.

Trim the bottom edge of a sweater with a single bias strip, either all left bias or all right bias. No zig zag. Starting at one side seam, measure the distance all around the edge to be trimmed. Knit a strip long enough to fit that measurement, and pin it all around the edge till the 2 short ends meet at the seam. Overcast the 2 short edges together with matching yarn. Overcast the bottom edge of the bias strip to the bottom edge of the sweater. Overcast the top edge of the bias to the sweater with neat, even stitches. Pull any loose ends to the wrong side and weave them in.

The sweater above shows a mini lightning strip used as a surface decoration.

20

Express Yourself

It's a given—everyone wears clothes (except nudists). People come in all sizes and shapes—short, tall, fat, skinny. Choosing appropriate clothing to fit your budget and figure, and blend with what you already have in your closet and still be in fashion, can be a monumental decision. We're all influenced by the magazines and newspapers; and television can blow your mind. Everything always looks great on those professional models. But we aren't all fashion models, and we can deceive ourselves.

Today there are few fashion restrictions, and most of you know enough to wear what seems comfortable and appropriate. Nevertheless, unless you have pots of money, changing your wardrobe just to keep up can be an expensive proposition—especially for those of you whose bodies may be shifting and changing.

An alternative to spending big bucks is to wear a basic sweater and doll it up with accessories. Wear two or three belts twisted together below your natural waistline. How about an oversize triangle scarf tied around, then tucked into the neckline?

Accessories, wisely chosen, can add zest to your wardrobe.

Knowing how to knit can open up a whole new world of individuality, without being too peculiar, and save you a bundle, too. Knitting is a practical craft. Although "practical" somehow brings forth images of dull and boring, it's not necessarily so. Practical may encourage you to plan ahead: to evaluate what's already hanging in your closet. More importantly, it can mean a fantastic wardrobe of sweaters, hats, scarves, or whatever else you can dream up. Your creativity will impress your friends. An additional bonus—when your fingers become more nimble with the needles and yarn, you could earn some extra money knitting for others.

The word "style" is overworked; yet it is too important to be ignored. Even in the early years, you are aware of the image you project to others. Your knowledge about clothes, make-up, and how you behave certainly influence how you feel about yourself.

Take a really close look at yourself in the mirror—from head to toe. Don't moan and groan. The truth hurts just for a little while. Are you one of the lucky ones who has no figure faults? Most of us aren't so fortunate.

We all have a figure problem we wish would disappear, or a figure "plus" that might be emphasized. Hand knits can help you both ways. They can keep you stylishly warm in winter, and cool and comfortable in summer.

Blousy sleeve

Are you self-conscious about your bust-line because it's too small—or too full? A fuzzy, soft, low-keyed mohair will help disguise your bust. A generous, fluid sweater can disguise you either way.

Try a blouson. It emphasizes slender hips and makes your legs look longer. It also will hide a fat tummy and other problem bulges. Make a longer blouson to hide thunder thighs.

Are narrow, sloping shoulders a problem? Try a dimpled or puffed sleeve for balance, and to give the illusion of broader shoulders. Insert shoulder pads for that Joan Crawford look. Focus attention away from your droopy shoulders to some other area above the waistline as a slenderizing trick.

Do you feel like a football player because you think your shoulders are too broad? Diminish the width with an undefined armhole (no shape). Because the shoulder line will slope naturally two or three inches below the natural shoulder, it deemphasizes the width.

Make sleeves work for you. A skin-tight sleeve will emphasize a heavy upper arm. A fuller sleeve, tight at the wrist, but puffy, will draw the eye away from the upper arm and focus interest at the wrist.

Upper arms too skinny? Use a bumpy, multicolored yarn. The interest will be on the yarn rather than your arm. It's all illusion. See how it works?

Stripes used properly as a focal point can direct the eye anywhere. Use them vertically, horizontally or diagonally to enliven a basic sweater. Knit stripes directly into the fabric of the sweater, or make them separately and stitch them on later.

Use narrow, contrasting stripes around the neckline or cuff and no one will ever notice a chunky waistline. Attach stripes horizontally from one armhole across the front and down the opposite side. Do you feel you're too tall? Place the stripes right at the waistline, or at the hip, then add a couple more on the sleeves.

Alternate stripes of two or more colors

Stripes as decorative details

Wrong side of stockinette knitted stripes

throughout the sweater. Pair the sweater with a matching or contrasting color skirt. Add a tailored shirt and there's a coordinated outfit. For dressier occasions, wear the sweater with some jewelry, or a pretty scarf.

Each time you plan a new sweater, try a different type of yarn with different size needles. Add another detail you've not tried before, or invent your own. This is how to add to your repertoire of knitting skills and at the same time acquaint yourself with new textures and more exotic yarns. Soon your fingers will begin to develop a sixth sense. Make color magic work with your new skills.

Convert that same basic pullover into a sweater dress. Make it grow. Decide the length, then make a note of the number of inches from the top of the shoulder down over the bustline to the hem. If your hips are larger than your bustline, add a couple of extra inches to the width measurement —and another inch for good luck. Multiply the number of stitches in the gauge by the number of inches across, and starting from the bottom, cast on that number and work straight up.

Wear an interesting belt at the waist, or around the hips, just for fun. Wear your sweater dress over your jeans or pants. Now think of other ways.

This is a time for experimenting—a time for change, and a time for developing a sense of yourself. Take off the rose-colored glasses and size yourself up honestly. Dress in the right way for your body!

21

Three and More for the Road

Measurements: Length, center back to hem —24 inches

Back width, side to side—23 inches

Materials: 4 3½ oz. skeins pink machine washable wool knitting worsted

4 3½ oz. skeins lavender machine washable wool knitting worsted

1 pair #10 knitting needles or size to obtain gauge

Crochet hook—size "G"

Tapestry needle

T-pins

Scissors

Gauge: 4 stitches = 1 inch

Back: With one color, cast on 50 stitches. Knit 1 row. On next row, increase 1 stitch

The knit designs in this chapter can be the foundation for a great wardrobe. Each was created to be worn in a variety of ways. They can be mixed and matched, and easily changed or altered. The knitting tricks you've already learned are included. Now it's time to step out on your own. Add or subtract stitches according to your measurements.

Reversible Bubble Vest

This is a reversible knitted version of the popular sleeveless down-filled vest. Actually, it's two vests connected with single crochet. The colors are soft pink and lavender, with one pocket on the outside and another on the inside, stitched to blend in with the bubbles. Make the vest from any 2 colors you please. No blocking is necessary.

Dana models reversible bubble vest

in every stitch (100 stitches). Purl next row. Work 4 inches even in stockinette stitch, or desired depth of bubble. End on purl side. On next row knit, decreasing (knit 2 together) across row (50 stitches). Knit next 3 rows. On next row, knit, increasing 1 stitch in every stitch (100 stitches). Work 4 more sections the same way, ending with knit decrease row. Knit 1 row. Bind off on next row.

Fronts: Make 2. Cast on 25 stitches for each front. Knit 1 row. On next row increase 1 stitch in every stitch (50 stitches). Purl next row. Work even in stockinette stitch for 4 inches (to match back). End on purl side. On next row, knit, decreasing (knit 2 together) across row (25 stitches).

Knit the next 3 rows. On next row, knit, increasing 1 stitch in every stitch (50 stitches). Work 4 more sections the same way, ending with knit decrease row. Knit 1 row. Bind off on next row.

For the reverse side, make the two fronts and back the same way.

Finishing: Weave in any loose ends (page 72). With right sides facing, place a pin 4½ inches in from each armhole edge and pin front and back shoulders of pink sections together. Carefully backstitch. For arm-

Detail—pinning two parts of bubble vest at armhole

Detail—bubble vest pocket

hole, place a T-pin 9 inches below shoulder seam. Pin, then sew side seams. Be sure that gathers meet neatly at side seam edges. Connect lavender sections the same way. Crochet pink side to lavender side with single crochet stitch (page 71). With *wrong* sides facing, pin all outside edges of both colors together, carefully matching gathers. With either pink or lavender, start single crochet at right shoulder seam through both edges at the same time. Single crochet all around neckline to left front edge. Work 3 single crochets in one stitch at corner. Continue down front to corner of front, work 3 single crochets in one stitch, continue single crochet across front and along back, working 3 single crochets at corner, crochet up right front, around neckline, back to beginning. Fasten off. Pull end of yarn through between the layers to wrong side.

Pin together, then single crochet around

each armhole edge. Fasten off. Pull end through between layers.

Pockets: Make two - 1 from each color.

Cast on 15 stitches. Make bubble as described for body of sweater, working to same depth. Bind off. In second bubble above sweater hem, on either left or right side, pin pocket at side seam, and carefully match top and bottom edges of pocket to bubble. Sew around 3 sides, leaving side edge free. Sew second pocket to reverse side. Pull loose ends through between layers.

Tie: Optional. Measure off 3 16-inch strands of yarn—2 pink, 1 lavender, or vice versa, and braid together. Make two. Firmly stitch one to each side of neckline. Weave loose ends back through braid.

Use any combination of colors for this sweater. Alternate colors for back and fronts, if you choose. Knit the vest to any desired length, but make widths of bubbles consistent. Sew the pockets to each right front, and alternate those colors. Add several sets of braided ties down center front. Use your imagination. Wear the Bubble Vest with a turtleneck or shirt.

Country Cousins

Twin sets are a wardrobe plus. Wear the long-sleeved pullover with or without its matching vest. Wear the sleeveless vest over a tailored shirt, with a T-shirt. Mix and match. The set shown here features a vertically-striped pullover with a companion wool tweed sleeveless vest. The body of the pullover is knitted side to side, alternating the tweed and solid stripes. The muted tweed enhances the solid stripes. Choose your own yarn combinations, or

make both sweaters all one color. The vertical stripes are slenderizing. Both yarns are medium weight wool, but knitted with larger needles.

Measurements: Bust (finished, seam to seam): 18 inches

Length (center back to hem): 24 inches

Sleeve length: 21 inches;

Upper arm: 18 inches.

Materials: Pullover: 3 2-oz. balls wool tweed, main color

2 2-oz. balls knitting worsted, color B

Tapestry needle

Crochet hook

T-pins

Tape measure

Row counter

Gauge: 3 stitches = 1 inch

Back: With main color, cast on 68 stitches. Beginning and ending *every* row with a knit stitch, work 14 rows in stockinette stitch. Change to color B, work 6 rows. 12 rows main color, 6 rows color B, 12 rows main color, 6 rows color B, 8 rows main color, 6 rows color B, and 6 rows main color. Bind off.

Front: Same as back.

Sleeves: Make two. With #9 needle and color B for cuff cast on 32 stitches and work 8 rows knit 1, purl 1 ribbing, 4 rows main color, 6 rows color B, 8 rows main color. Continue in ribbing, working 4 more rows. Change to color B and to larger needle. On next row, in stockinette stitch, increase 10 stitches evenly spaced

Dana relaxes in vertical-striped pullover.
Yarn courtesty of Tinctoria.

The same sweater worn with a belt

along the row (42 stitches). Work 6 rows color B. Continue in stockinette stitch, alternating 12 rows main color and six rows color B, increasing 1 stitch at beginning and end of row every 1½ inches 8 times (58 stitches). Work even until sleeve measures 21 inches, or desired length. End with main color. Bind off. For a shorter sleeve, knit fewer stripes, or make them narrower. Be sure that both sleeves match.

Ribbed Hem: With smaller needles and main color, turn work so that stripes are vertical, starting at right edge. Pick up 68 stitches evenly spaced. Work 2½ inches in knit 1, purl 1 ribbing. Bind off loosely in pattern. Work the same on back.

Sewing up: Shoulders: With wrong sides facing, pin front and back shoulders together. Place T-pin at outer edges, and at 4½ inches in on each side. Matching stripes, backstitch each shoulder. Turn work to right side. With smaller needle, pick up 34 stitches evenly spaced between

Picked-up ribbed stitches at sweater hem

Neckline of vertical-striped pullover

shoulder seams for neck band. Work even in stockinette stitch for 1½ inches. End on wrong side. On next knit row, knit in back of every stitch for a turning row. Knitting in the back of each stitch forms a row of flat twisted stitches that will serve as a guideline for the neckline hem. Knit 1¼ inches. Bind off loosely. Work same on second piece.

Sew sleeves to armholes. Sew underarm and side in one long seam. Fold neckband to wrong side at turning row and slip stitch. Weave in loose ends. Lightly press seams on wrong side.

Sleeveless Vest

Back: With #11 needle, working from bottom hem to shoulder, cast on 70 stitches. Work in knit 1, purl 1 ribbing for about 2½ inches. On next row, in stockinette stitch, increase 1 stitch at beginning and end of row and continue working even until piece measures about 20 inches (or desired length to underarm).

Armhole: Bind off 5 stitches at the beginning of next 2 rows, decrease 1 stitch at beginning and end of next row. The bound-off stitches form the base of the armhole—the decrease stitches slightly shape it. Continue even until armhole measures 8 inches. Bind off.

Pocket Lining: Make two. With #9 needle, cast on 12 stitches and work in stockinette stitch for 3 inches. End on purl row. Break yarn and slip to holder.

Left Front: (Right side facing you) cast on 36 stitches. Work 32 stitches in ribbing, and last 4 stitches in garter stitch (border). End on wrong side. At beginning of next

row, increase 1 stitch, work 32 stitches, knit 1, purl 1 ribbing, and last 4 stitches in garter stitch. Continue in pattern, working 4 stitches in garter stitch border at center edge.

Insert Pockets: When work measures 6 inches, work across 12 stitches, bind off next 12 stitches, finish row. On next row (wrong side) work 12 stitches. Work 12 stitches from holder on purl side. Complete row. When work measures 20 inches, bind off for armhole (same as back). Work even until armhole measures 8 inches. Bind off loosely.

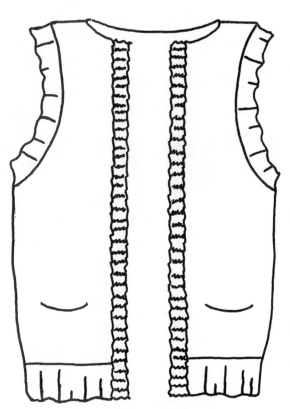

Sleeveless country cousin vest.
Yarn courtesy of Tinctoria.

Right Front: Same as left front, but reverse pattern and armhole shaping. Work pocket same as left front.

Sewing up: With right sides facing, sew shoulder seams. Turn to right side. Starting at right armhole edge, with #9 needle, pick up 82 stitches around armhole and work in ribbing for 1½ inches. Bind off. On wrong side, slip stitch pocket linings (page 56). Sew side seams. Lightly press seams and pocket linings on wrong side. Work one row single crochet around neckline and pocket openings. Weave in loose ends.

Striped, Rolled-Neck Sweater, Miniskirt

Sweater:
   Size: Bust—33 inches, 16½ inches from side seam to side seam. Shoulder to hem—17½ inches. Armhole—8 inches, shoulder to underarm. Sleeve (before hemming)—7½ inches.

Skirt: Waist—about 26 inches
   Length—waist to hem (finished)—26 inches

Materials: 2 colors, 4 each, blue and yellow, 4 oz. skeins or balls wool knitting worsted. Elastic for sleeves and waist.
   #8 and #10 knitting needles (or size to obtain gauge)
   Tapestry needle
   Crochet hook
   Scissors
   Tape measure
   Row counter

Gauge: 4 stitches = 1 inch

Dana wearing sprightly striped sweater and mini-skirt

Sweater Back: With smaller needle and blue, cast on 68 stitches. Work 3 inches in reverse knit 1, purl 1 ribbing. Change to larger needles, increase 1 stitch at beginning and end of next row (70 stitches). Work even in stockinette stitch for 3 inches. Change to yellow, and work 12 rows even, 6 rows blue, 6 rows yellow, 4 rows blue, 10 rows yellow, 2 rows blue, 12 rows yellow, 12 rows blue, 6 rows yellow. Bind off loosely.

Sweater Front: Same as back.

Sleeves: Make two. With larger needle and yellow, starting at armhole edge, cast on 64 stitches. Work 12 rows even in stockinette stitch, 2 rows blue, 6 rows yellow, 4 rows blue, 10 rows yellow, 4 rows blue, 10 rows yellow, ending on purl side. On next row, knit in back of every stitch. (This is turning row for hem.) Purl next row. Work 4 more rows stockinette stitch. Bind off.

Miniskirt Back: With blue and smaller needles, cast on 60 stitches. Work 6 rows even in stockinette stitch. End with purl row. On next row, knit in back of every stitch. Purl 1 row. Continue in stockinette stitch for 6 rows. Change to larger needle, and work 6 more rows. Work 4 rows yellow, 10 rows blue. Still working with blue, on next knit row, increase 1 stitch in every stitch on row (120 stitches). Purl back. Work 4 rows yellow, 12 rows blue, 4 rows yellow, 12 rows blue, 4 rows yellow, 12 rows blue, 4 rows yellow, 8 rows blue. End on purl row. On next row, knit in back of every stitch (turning row for hem). Purl back. Work 4 more rows blue. Bind off.

Front: Same as back.

Finishing: Sweater: Leave 8-inch opening for neck, and with right sides facing, backstitch front and back shoulders together. Backstitch sleeves to armholes. Sew side seams, matching up stripes (Connections pages 66–72). Fold sleeve hem at turning row to wrong side, and slip-stitch in place.

Leave small opening to insert elastic (optional). Weave in all loose ends on wrong side.

Rolled Collar: With right side facing and smaller needles, pick up and knit 35 stitches evenly spaced across front neck opening. Work even in stockinette stitch for 2 inches. Bind off loosely. Work the same way for back neck opening. Overcast 2 short ends at each side.

Finishing Skirt: Pin and sew side seams, matching stripes. Fold top to wrong side on reverse knitted row for casing, and slip-stitch loosely. Leave a small opening to insert elastic. Fold hem to wrong side at reversed knitted row, and slip-stitch loosely. Weave in loose ends on wrong side. If necessary, lightly moisten and flatten seams with palm of hand on wrong side. Let dry completely.

Variations: You may alternate stripes in any sequence you please. Or use only one color for skirt and sweater. If you prefer long sleeves, buy 2 more balls of yarn. Start the sleeve from the cuff and work in reverse knit 1, purl 1 ribbing to match sweater hem. Or eliminate ribbing and insert elastic at wrist for gathered sleeve.

To make the skirt longer, continue knitting even to the desired length, adding additional stripes as you want. Let me remind you again, reduce or increase the number of stitches to fit your own measurements.

Body-Hugging Ribbed Sweater Jacket

This close-to-the-body wool sweater jacket has a ribbed body with stockinette sleeves and ribbed neckline. It is made

Body hugging ribbed sweater jacket

from a varicolored bulky handspun wool in shades of magenta, delphinium, red, brown and toast, with a slender black thread interwoven throughout and is another variation of the classic cardigan. Two strands of knitting worsted weight yarn may be substituted: use one color if you want a solid color sweater and 2 colors knit together for a different tweedy look.

Measurements: Back (shoulder to shoulder) —22 inches; Sleeve length—20 inches, including 4½-inch cuff; Center back to hem—19 inches.

Materials: 4 4–oz. skeins extra bulky wool (approx. 120 yards per skein) or 3 4-oz. skeins knitting worsted doubled.
   #11 and #13 knitting needles, (or size to obtain gauge)
   Crochet hook
   Stitch holders
   Tapestry needle
   Tape measure
   T-pins
Gauge: 2 stitches = 1 inch
   Back: With #11 needles, cast on 48 stitches. Work in knit 1, purl 1 ribbing for 5½ inches. On next row, change to #13

needles. Continuing in ribbing, increase 1 stitch at beginning and end of next row. Work even in pattern until piece measures 19 inches or desired length. Bind off loosely in pattern.

Left Front: (Right side facing you) with #11 needles, cast on 26 stitches. Work in knit 1 purl 1 ribbing, for 5½ inches, placing markers for buttons on 3rd stitch from end of row on 3rd row, and every 16th row, until there are 5 markers. At same time, when work measures 5½ inches, change to #13 needles, and continue in ribbing until piece measures 17 inches. Work across to within 8 stitches of end of row. Slip remaining 8 stitches to stitch holder. Turn work and decrease 1 stitch at neck edge, every *other* row twice; continue even in ribbing until work measures 19 inches. Bind off loosely in pattern.

Right Front: (left side facing you) with #11 needles, cast on 26 stitches. Work to correspond to left front, making 2-stitch buttonhole (page 87) on 3rd row (2 stitches in from center edge), and every 16th row, until there are 5 buttonholes. At center neck, work 8 stitches and slip them onto a stitch holder. Decrease 1 stitch at neck edge every other row twice; continue even in ribbing until piece matches other side. Bind off loosely in pattern.

Sleeves: (Make two) With smaller needle, cast on 20 stitches and work even in knit 1, purl 1 ribbing for 4 inches. On next row, change to #13 needles, and working in stockinette stitch, increase 8 stitches evenly spaced across row. Continue in stockinette stitch, working even, until sleeve measures 20 inches, or desired length. Bind off loosely.

Sewing up: With right sides facing, pin, then sew shoulder seams with finer weight wool. Sew sleeves to armholes. Sew underarm and sleeve seams. Overcast or buttonhole stitch with finer yarn around buttonholes. Lightly press seams.

Neck Ribbing: With smaller needle, starting at right center edge, working from right side out, knit first 8 stitches from holder, pick up 44 stitches evenly spaced around neckline, knit remaining 8 stitches from other holder. Work 1 inch knit 1, purl 1 ribbing. Bind off loosely in pattern.

Sew on buttons at markers after seams have been pressed.

22

Tender, Loving Care

Hand knits, or any knits for that matter, need tender, loving care to hold their shape and stay fresh and bright.

After each wearing, turn the sweater inside out and let it rest awhile before putting it away. Yarns absorb body odors. They are especially susceptible to colognes and perfumes. Deodorants are particularly destructive. When you don't plan to wear a blouse or shirt under the sweater, to preserve the fibers wear a pair of *cotton* dress shields (no plastic).

Dust loves yarns. To protect them, wrap your knits in a length of muslin that's been laundered several times. An old cotton pillow case will do as well. NEVER, NEVER store knits in sealed plastic bags. The plastic doesn't breathe, and the moisture may produce mildew, which will harm the fibers.

Is it better to wash or dry clean knits? I've been asked this question hundreds of times, and my answer is always a firm "wash." Man-made or synthetic yarns, especially, should *not* be dry cleaned. They absorb the cleaning solvent odors, which almost never go away. The hot steam from the presser will totally relax, and sometimes melt, the synthetic yarns. One sweater down the drain! Wools will also absorb some of the solvent odor, particularly if the solvent has been reused many times. Who's to know? There's no assurance that the solvent is fresh.

Hand washing is the most satisfactory cleaning method for soiled or dull knits. So it's time to recheck the yarn label for the manufacturer's washing instructions. Read it carefully. Although hand washing may take a little more time and effort, your sweater will stay fresh and soft, and the colors will retain their brightness. While it's still damp, an out-of-shape wool sweater may be manipulated and wiggled back to the original shape because wool has a "memory."

Cotton and linen yarns wash beautifully. Laundering renews the fibers, which may then be steam pressed without damage. Handle these yarns as you would any woven cotton or linen material.

There's a specific difference between that first blocking immediately after you've finished knitting your sweater and the blocking you'll do after the sweater has been worn many times. For example: the sweater is finished and you can hardly wait to show it off. Hold it a minute! The body of the sweater won't require much attention, but the seams should be lightly blocked. Here's how: turn the sweater to the wrong side and lay a moistened press-

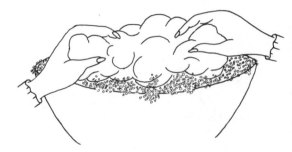

Washing sweater

ing cloth (a scrap of toweling will do) on top of the seam. Hold the steam iron just above the seam. Skim over the cloth and rotate the iron. *Don't press hard.* With the palm of your other hand press down on the seam. Turn the sweater to the right side and let it dry thoroughly.

Assuming it fits properly, lay the sweater on a large sheet of white paper and draw an outline of it. Use only a *pencil*—no marking pen or ball point because the ink might run off onto the material, and you know it's almost impossible to remove that stuff. Keep this outline as a permanent record of the original shape. *Don't forget where it is.*

OK. You've worn your sweater many times and now it's ready to be washed. Get out that original outline and lay the sweater on top of it. Does it match the original shape, or has it stretched out? Don't cry—you'll be able to wiggle it back after you've washed it.

To begin, trace that first outline onto another sheet of paper and save the original. Place a large bath towel underneath the new outline and keep it nearby. Now you're ready to wash.

Fill the sink (I always use the bathroom or kitchen sink) with cool or lukewarm water, and add a capful of liquid soap (no detergent). Whip up some suds. Turn your sweater inside out and carefully place it in the sudsy water. Squish the sweater around in the suds *(no wringing)* for a minute or so. Rinse carefully in two or three changes of water, or until the last rinse water is clear.

Drain the water from the sink, then squeeze and press out as much remaining water as possible. With both hands lift the sweater, lay it out on another clean bath towel. and roll it up. Do something else for an hour or so while the towel absorbs more of the moisture.

Unroll the towel and gently lift the sweater onto the paper outline. Shift it around until it matches the pencil drawing. Press it out with your hands. This will help to smooth out the knit material so it will be ready to wear after it dries.

After a few hours, turn the sweater to the other side in order for air to circulate through the material. By now the paper outline will be icky wet, and you can toss it out. Let the sweater dry on the towel for a few hours. Turn it right side out, place it on a clean, *dry* towel and use your hands to press it again. If the sweater is made from a very thick wool, it may have to be turned once or twice more before it's completely dry.

Two important laundering "don'ts." Don't put your wool sweater in the dryer; don't hang it in the sun.

Does it seem like a lot of trouble? Perhaps someone in your family could be persuaded to help. I can assure you this extra attention pays off.

Avoid abusing your knits. Keep them looking fresh and ready to wear at a moment's notice. Don't toss them in a drawer or hang them on a wire coat hanger. Stuff the sleeves with tissue paper or clean rags, tuck some tissue between the folds to prevent creasing, then fold them neatly. Admittedly, I haven't always taken my own advice—you know, "Don't do as I do, do as I say." My carelessness only wasted time, and at the last minute there I'd be, steaming out wrinkles. Better to be prepared.

23

Something New from Something Old

In these days of high prices and complicated technology, it's wasteful to throw anything away if it can be reused. And that's the beauty of hand knitting. It's a simple matter to take your tired old sweater apart and use the yarn over again. If the idea of unraveling turns you off, let me encourage you to learn how, because, although it may seem grueling, think of the dollars you'll save, and you'll have something new in the bargain.

The already-knitted yarn may lose a bit of its original elasticity, but it's not enough to worry about. You may forfeit some yardage, however. Take advantage of the opportunity to tap your creativity and invent a completely different design. Probably there will be sufficient yarn to at least make the front and back of a sweater, but you may have to buy a couple of balls of similar yarn if some radical design changes are intended. Anyway, here's how to recycle.

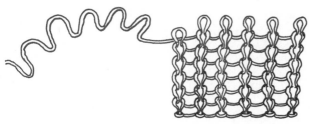

Unraveling yarn

it off. Take care not to wind too firmly because it puts extra strain on the used yarn.

When all the unraveling and "hanking" are done, wash the yarn just as you would a sweater (page 106). Give all the hanks a quick roll in a bath towel to remove extra water, then hang the hanks on padded or terry-covered hangers. If you don't have padded hangers, drape the hanks round all the faucets in the bathtub. It may take a day or so for the yarn to dry thoroughly, so be patient.

When you're sure the yarn is dry, wind it loosely back into balls, and you'll be on your way ready to start your next creation.

Remember that I encouraged you to leave little traffic signs on the inside of your sweater to remind you where to start the unraveling process? Turn the sweater to the wrong side and identify where you finished sewing the last seam. Think in reverse. Start at the bottom of one seam and tug until you can see the stitching. With your tapestry needle, remove the anchor stitch (don't cut it). Pick out each stitch until one side is separated from the other. Do the same on the opposite side. Next, remove the armhole stitchings, and finally, the shoulder stitchings. Now you're ready to unravel.

Before you use the yarn again, it should be washed. To do that, wind it into hanks as you unravel.

With the right side of the material facing you, find the last bound-off stitch of one shoulder. It should be at the left side.

As you unravel, wind the yarn around a large piece of cardboard or a big dictionary. Wind each section into a separate hank, to remind you how much yarn was originally used for each part. With cotton string, tie each hank in a few places and slip

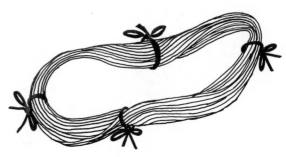

Wound in hank

24

Bits and Pieces

Those leftover yarns you've been accumulating need not go to waste. They can be used to make all kinds of very wearable and useful things such as hodgepodge sweaters, hats, scarves, leg warmers, pillows. Now that you've learned what makes knitting tick, get going. For starters, here are a few patterns you might like to try.

Hodgepodge Hat and Scarf

This hat and scarf were knitted with small amounts of 8 different colors and textures of wool left over from previous projects. Each color section ended at the seam, so that when the hat was sewn, the stripes matched as closely as possible. However, it really doesn't make much difference. You may choose to start a new color anywhere you please.

Hat: Measure the circumference of your head. Average width for this type of hat is about 17 inches. Select the first color and work a swatch of that yarn for a stitch gauge. My gauge was 5 stitches to the inch. The wool yarn was comparable to knitting worsted, knitted with #9 needles (page 31). Cast on the appropriate number of stitches (17 inches multiplied by 5 equals 85 stitches) and work in stockinette stitch

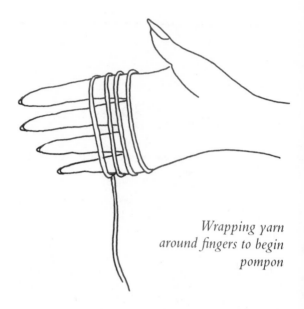

Wrapping yarn around fingers to begin pompon

(changing colors when you feel like it) for 2 inches. At the same time, decrease 1 stitch at the beginning and end of a row every 1½ inches. Work in garter stitch for 2 inches, then change back to stockinette stitch. Continue decreasing as described, but when hat measures 5 inches, work 1 inch in garter stitch. When vertical measurement is 8 inches from the beginning, decrease 1 stitch every *4th stitch.* Purl back. Decrease 1 stitch every *other* stitch across the row. Continue decreasing *every other stitch* on *every knit row* until there are 6 or 8 stitches remaining. Cut the yarn about 18 to 20 inches from the needle. You will use this to gather the top and sew the seam. Thread the yarn onto your tapestry needle and weave the needle through the loops on the knitting needle. Remove the knitting needle and pull the loops together. Weave in and out over that last stitch. Turn to wrong side. Pin the side edges together, then backstitch the two edges together carefully. Trim the bottom of the hat with a narrow bias band.

Bias Band: With any color, using #9 needles, cast on 6 stitches. Work in bias (page 90) until band is long enough to fit around bottom edge of hat. Bind off. Sew the 2 short edges together. Pin band to bottom edge, starting at seam. With matching yarn, overcast bottom edge, then the top edge. Needs no blocking.

Pompon: The pompon on the hat is also optional. It was made with all the colors used for the hat. Here's an easy way to make a pompon. Cut a 10-inch length of any color, and set it aside. Loosely wind your yarn around 4 fingers until you have a fat bunch. As one color ends, start another. When the pompon is as thick as you want, cut the yarn. Slide the wrapped yarn off your fingers. Pick up the 10-inch strand of yarn and wrap it tightly around the middle of the bunch, 4 or 5 times, and tie a knot. There will be a long end. With your scissors, cut the loops on each side.

Turn the hat wrong side out and pull the long end of the yarn through the hole on top. Thread it onto your tapestry needle and sew in and out through the gathered stitches. Fasten off. Weave the cut end through the seam on the wrong side. Fluff up the pompon with your fingers, and trim any straggly edges. For a fluffier pompon, boil some water in a saucepan and hold the pompon over the pan. Give it a few turns so the steam penetrates all around. Shake the hat a few times to remove any moisture, then place the hat over a tall glass until the pompon is completely dry. It won't take long.

Scarf: The scarf measures 8 inches across and 52 inches long without fringe, but you can make it any width and length you please, depending on the amount of yarn there is. Multiply the number of inches by the number of stitches in your gauge (mine was 5 stitches to the inch), so I cast on 40 stitches. To make the side edges stay flat, knit the first and last stitch of every row, and work in-between stitches in stockinette stitch. Change colors whenever you please. The colors are not necessarily in the same order as in the hat. Change to garter stitch if you want to. You may make your scarf wider or narrower, shorter or longer. The fringe is optional. I fringed this scarf because I still had a few odds and ends left over and wanted to use them up.

Fringe: The fringe on this scarf is a 4-strand fringe, or 2 strands of yarn folded in half. The finished length is 2 inches. You can make your fringe any length or thick-

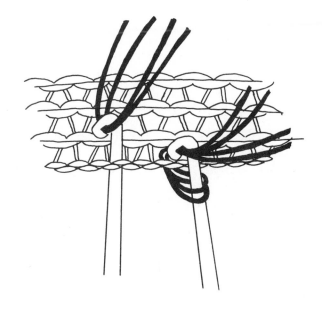

Attaching fringe

Fringe attached to skirt hem (detail)

ness. A single strand of yarn makes a 2-strand fringe, so decide on the thickness and spacing before you cut the yarn.

Cut a piece of firm cardboard about 2 inches wide and 3½ inches long. For each 4-strand fringe, wrap the yarn around the cardboard twice. This scarf is edged with 33 fringes. For that number, wrap the yarn around the cardboard 66 times, and cut the yarn. Cut the yarn across the bottom of the card. To attach the fringe, hold two strands together and fold them in half. With the right side facing you, put your crochet hook through the stitch where you intend to connect the fringe. Catch both strands with the hook and pull them through halfway. This makes a large loop. Now pull the ends of the yarn through the loop. One loop has been fastened. Make one fringe in every other stitch along one edge, and do the same on the other edge. Alternate colors, or use two colors for each fringe. After you have attached all the fringes, give each one a little pull. This will anchor the yarn. If the edges look a little ragged, trim them with your scissors.

Striped leg warmers from odds and ends

Hodgepodge Leg Warmers

There are 5 colors in these leg warmers, because those are the ones that happened to be at the bottom of my knitting bag. These were knitted with a #9 needle, and a stitch gauge of 5 stitches to the inch. The finished width at the ankle is 8 inches and the top

measures 12 inches. You may need to add or subtract stitches according to your own measurements and stitch gauge. Leg warmers do not require a precise fit, so a stitch or two, more or less, is no big deal. The length from top to bottom is about 24 inches. This, too, is up to you.

Cast on 40 stitches. Work in reverse knit 1, purl 1 ribbing for about 3 inches. Change to stockinette stitch, increase 1 stitch at beginning and end of next row, and about every 1½ inches on a knit row,

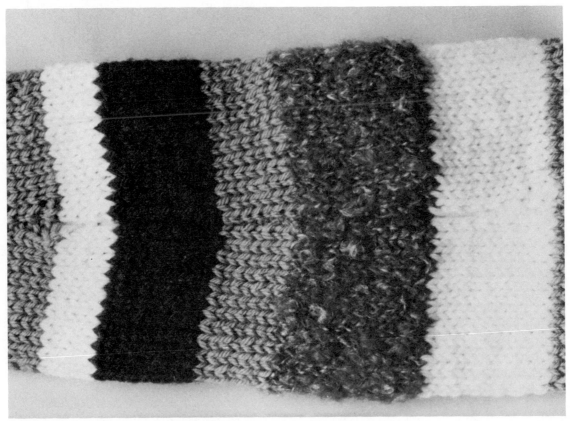

Matching stripes on leg warmers (detail)

until knitting measures about 24 inches, or desired length, working last 4 inches in reverse rib. Bind off loosely in pattern. Make two.

Sewing up: Fold the two long edges in half with right sides facing. Pin the two edges together, matching stripes carefully. Use plenty of pins. Thread the major color through the tapestry needle and backstitch very close to edge. If necessary, work elastic thread through top cuff, to keep it from sliding. No blocking necessary. Enjoy!

Doggy Duds

Even doggies wear sweaters. Here's a nifty sweater you can knit in a couple of days. If you have some odds and ends you want to use, this is one way. This sweater is made from machine-washable acrylic knitting worsted, trimmed with a multicolor yarn of a comparable weight. Make several as gifts for your dog-lover friends.

Materials: 1 2-oz. skein knitting worsted for main color. Turtle neck and trim: 1 oz. multicolor knitting worsted
   #9 needles
   Crochet hook
   Tapestry needle
Gauge: 4 stitches = 1 inch

With multicolored yarn, cast on 45 stitches. Work in knit 1, purl 1 ribbing for 4 inches. On next row, with main color, increase 4 stitches evenly spaced across row (49 stitches). Continue in stockinette stitch, placing markers 13 stitches from each edge. Work 4 rows even.

On next row, work to marker, slip marker to right needle, knit 1, increase 1 stitch, work until 2 stitches remain before marker, increase 1 stitch, knit 1, slip marker to right needle. Complete row. Purl next row. Repeat the increase row as described, every other row 7 times (63 stitches). Work even until 3 inches from ribbing.

Divide for legs: Work to first marker, join new yarn, work to second marker, join

Doggy Duds made by Betty Bell—front view

new yarn, work to end of row. Drop markers. Work each piece separately, work even until 2 inches from dividing row. Work all the way across, dropping extra balls. Work even until piece measures 7 inches from ribbing, or desired length for dog's chest.

Shaping: Bind off 13 stitches at beginning of next two rows. Decrease 1 stitch each side every *other* row 5 times, decrease 1 stitch *every* row 4 times. *Bind off* 3 stitches *every* row 4 times. Bind off remaining stitches.

Sewing up: With right sides facing, back-stitch chest seam as close to edge as possible. Work 1 row of single crochet around bottom edge, and around each paw opening.

side view

back view

25

Knitting to Decorate

Knitting isn't just for wearing on your body. It can also be used to make decorative things for your home. Knit a patchwork throw rug to keep beside the bed. How about a curtain for a window, a bunch of pillows for your bed, or even a crazy hanging to put on a wall? Here are some easy designs for you to try.

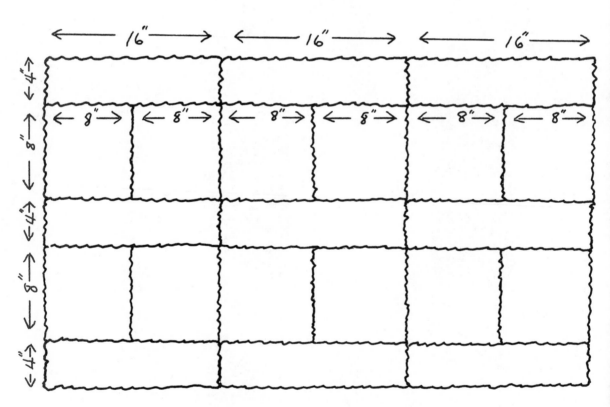

Diagram of patchwork rug

Patchwork Rug

Materials: 6 4-oz. skeins knitting worsted,
2 each of 3 different colors
1 2-oz. skein connecting color
1 pair #9 knitting needles
1 medium-size crochet hook
Tapestry needle
Scissors
Measurements: approximately 28 inches by
48 inches
Gauge: 5 stitches = 1 inch (gauge isn't crucial for this pattern)

Make 4 squares each of 3 main colors.
Cast on 40 stitches. Work 8 inches even in
garter stitch. Bind off. Make 3 rectangles
each of 3 main colors. Cast on 20 stitches.
Work 16 inches even in garter stitch. Bind
off. Lay out pieces according to diagram
on page 116, or create your own color
plan. Pin all parts together, and baste. With
connecting color, *slip stitch crochet* together.
To finish off, work 1 row single crochet all
around edge with connecting color. Be
sure to work 3 single crochets in each corner. Turn to wrong side and weave in all
loose ends.

This rug may also be used as a mini-
afghan. To make it larger, add more
squares and rectangles in any direction.

Window Curtain

Make a lacy curtain for your window with
medium-thick cotton string and #11
needles. Measure the length and width of
your window. Make a stitch gauge and
cast on twice the number of stitches as the
width measurement.

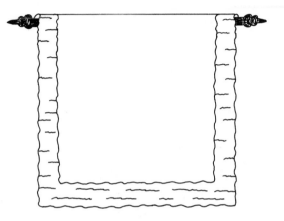

*Diagram of window curtain. Center area may
be any pattern stitch or all stockinette stitch.*

Example: For a window 26 inches wide,
with a stitch gauge of 3 stitches = 1 inch,
you would cast on 156 stitches. Work in
garter stitch (or any pattern stitch you
choose) until piece is desired length of window, plus 3 more inches for top casing.
Bind off.

To make side borders, no matter what
pattern stitch you plan to use, work the
first and last 10 stitches of *every* row in
garter stitch. Knit the beginning 10 rows
in garter stitch.

Casing: Fold the top (bind-off row) over
to wrong side (1½ inches) and slip stitch.
If you work in garter stitch, there is no
right or wrong side. Slide onto curtain rod.
This needs no pressing—it's all ready to
hang.

Bouquet of Pillows

A bunch of these mini-pillows make attractive decorations. From 1 4-oz. skein each of two colors, you will be able to make two pillows, including fringe, with a little bit left over. The colors used for the pillows in the photos are kelly green and pink. The diamond-shaped pillow is 10 inches on each side. The jellyroll pillow is 6 inches by 14½ inches. The stitch gauge is 4 stitches to the inch.

DIAMOND MINI PILLOW

Make 1 of each color. Start at one corner and cast on 3 stitches. Working in garter stitch, *increase* 1 stitch at beginning and end

Diamond mini pillow—pink side

green side

of *every other* row, until there are 53 stitches. Work in reverse, *decreasing* 1 stitch at beginning and end of *every other* row until there are 3 stitches remaining. Bind off. With either color, slip stitch crochet the two pieces together around 3 edges. Remember to crochet 3 stitches in one at each corner. Leave yarn attached. Stuff with foam rubber cut to size. Crochet remaining edges together and fasten off. Pull cut end of yarn to inside with your crochet hook. If you still have enough yarn left over, attach a double fringe around all 4 sides.

JELLYROLL PILLOW

Instead of two identical pillows, you can make the little diamond pillow and a jelly-roll pillow. Add some stripes or make each side a solid color. The stitch gauge is the same as the diamond pillow. The pink side was knitted vertically in stockinette stitch, and the other side was knitted horizontally in garter stitch.

Side 1: Cast on 24 stitches. Work even in stockinette stitch, adding stripes if desired, until piece measures 14½ or 15 inches.

Jelly roll pillow—striped side

solid color side

Side 2: Cast on 58 stitches. Work 6 inches even in garter stitch. Bind off. With either color, slip stitch around 3 outside edges (same as Diamond pillow). Stuff with foam rubber cut to size. Crochet remaining edge. Fasten off. Pull cut end to wrong side. Again, fringing is optional.

Make some of these little pillows as gifts, or make a whole bunch of them for yourself. Both pillows were photographed before stuffing to give you a bird's eye view of the process.

Wall Hanging

Now that you know the "how" and the "why", make something to hang on your wall. Use increasing and decreasing to knit a crazy shape. Add another color whenever you want to; include a pattern stitch or two. You can plan this project before you start, but you may find it more fun to just let it happen. That's what I do. Counting stitches isn't necessary, either, and your stitch gauge won't matter.

26
The End and the Beginning

It was my intention, with this book, to help clear away the cobwebs that mask this creative, satisfying and rediscovered craft of knitting. Throughout all my own years of enjoyment, I constantly discovered ways to do things that books didn't tell me. You'll never know unless you try. And it's true!

There are many techniques not described in this book. This was deliberate. I've tried to tell you about all the things I felt would be *most important* to you as a beginner and to invite you to use your intelligence. Are there other questions you'd like answered? Please write me in care of Atheneum Publishers.

I hope the curtain has parted enough to give you a peek at all the possibilities open to you. As I promised, once you understand the "why" and "how," the rest is all a matter of doing.

Dana Steele, a Campfire Horizon Club member in Seattle, is a perfect example of a beginner expanding her knitting horizons. Her first sweater (on page 122) was

Dana shows off her very first sweater

The sweaters and other projects described purposely did not always include specific measurements, so that you would be encouraged to adapt the design to fit you. It's all based on simple arithmetic. Do you have a home computer? Feed the information into the computer and let it do the work for you. Use the designs as guides; then go on to greater and more elaborate creations of your own.

This is the end of the book, but, I hope, the beginning of knitting for you.

made from knitting worsted, but even then she added her own special touch to a basic pullover by alternating rows of garter with rows of stockinette stitch. Her second sweater (frontis) was entirely her design, even to shaping the neckline and armholes. She has nearly finished a third project—a sleeveless, patterned vest. The front (on page 123) has an overall argyle pattern, made from cotton on #4 needles. The back is solid color. Dana conquered the intricacies of working with three colors, following a commercial pattern, only after several tries. Her tenacity paid off. When everything finally worked, she became a bona fide "knitaholic." I hope this success story will be an incentive for you.

Dana's pattern—detail

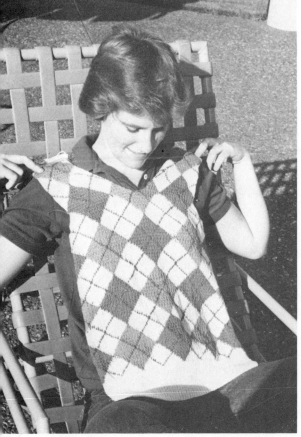

Dana's argyle vest

Dana's argyle pattern—detail

Index